A CENTURY UNDER SAIL

A CENTURY

Under Sail

SELECTED PHOTOGRAPHS BY *Morris Rosenfeld and Stanley Rosenfeld,*
legendary photographers of the America's Cup races

Text by Stanley Rosenfeld

ADDISON-WESLEY PUBLISHING COMPANY

Reading, Massachusetts · Menlo Park, California · New York
Don Mills, Ontario · Wokingham, England · Amsterdam · Bonn
Sydney · Singapore · Tokyo · Madrid · San Juan

The cover illustration of *Yankee* and *Rainbow* is one of six images reproduced in this book that are from the limited-edition portfolio of eight photographic prints entitled "The Tradition of America's Cup Racing."

This edition has been updated and expanded to include the trials and races for the 1987 America's Cup.

Library of Congress Cataloging-in-Publication Data

Rosenfeld, Morris, 1884–1968.
  A century under sail; selected photographs / by Morris Rosenfeld
and Stanley Rosenfeld; text by Stanley Rosenfeld.
    p. cm.
  Includes index.
  ISBN 0-201-07963-1
    1. Yachts and yachting—Pictorial works. 2. Sailing—Pictorial
works. 3. Rosenfeld, Morris, 1884–1968. 4. Rosenfeld, Stanley,
1913– . 5. Photographers—United States—Biography.
I. Rosenfeld, Stanley, 1913– . II. Title.
GV821.R67 1988   797.1′022′2—dc19   88-14626

The text and jacket of A CENTURY UNDER SAIL were designed by Janis Capone. The text was set in 10- and 12-point Sabon by DEKR Corp. of Woburn, Massachusetts. The display type, Centaur, was supplied by Williams Graphics of Wakefield, Massachusetts. Camera work, printing, and binding of the text and duotone illustrations were supplied by Arcata Graphics Halliday, Hanover, MA. The book is printed on 70-pound Warrenflo stock supplied by Lindenmeyr Paper Company of Boston, MA.

ABCDEFGHIJ-HA-898
First Printing, July 1988

To sailors and their craft.
Without them, these illustrations would be lonely sky and water.

Acknowledgments

With appreciation and gratitude . . .

To my late wife, Ruth Rosenfeld, who made it possible and reasonable and pleasurable for me to spend these many years afloat.

To Cherie Tripp, whose belief, regard, and enthusiasm for the Rosenfeld Collection are a vitalizing force.

To Heather Hanley, who discovered for us the Kaypro/WordStar connection and whose diligence and dedication helped bring these words to paper.

To Genoa Shepley, whose vision, planning, persistence, gourmet contributions, and editorial skill initiated and sustained this project.

Contents

Foreword · xi

Introduction · 3

PART ONE

Gaff-Riggers and Schooners, 1884–1929 · 13

PART TWO

The Magnificent Js, 1930–1937 · 59

PART THREE

Flying Spinnakers, 1938–1964 · 125

PART FOUR

On the Wind, 1965–1983 · 193

PART FIVE

Strong Winds Down Under, 1984–1987 · 253

Index · 277

Foreword

No history of American yachting would be complete without the story of the Rosenfeld clan and their work. From the beginning with Patriarch Morris through the latest artistry of son Stanley, their contributions to the visual record of our yachting heritage have been spectacular. Their work not only has been a documentary of the century on the waterfront, but has represented with great genius the sensitivity, the understanding, and the knowledge they have had of their subject matter.

I have been fortunate enough to know the Rosenfelds for as long as I can remember, but I must admit that my feeling of closeness to Stanley and particular appreciation of his warmth and humor stem from an incident in 1958. On a darkening, cold, late September afternoon at the Pelham Street dock in Newport, Rhode Island, the *Vim* crew manned the rail to await the arrival of the "Black Maria," the America's Cup Committee Boat, which we knew was on the way to eliminate us from further competition, and justly so. That afternoon we had lost the final trial race against *Columbia* and found ourselves to be on the short end of a four to two score. Even though we knew the end was inevitable, it was an unhappy moment. Harry Morgan's Cup Committee with Mike Vanderbilt, Percy Chubb, Burr Bartram, George Hinman, Luke Lockwood, W. A. W. Stewart, now all gone, arrived promptly. Our wonderful and great crew—Don and Dick Matthews, Ted Hood, Brad Noyes, Jakob Isbrandtsen, Buddy Bombard, Dick Bertram, Larry Sheu, Willy Carstens, et al.—stood at the rail to receive the thanks of the committee, drained, cold, and tired. As the Cup Committee Boat departed, all the crew had tears running down their cheeks and were in no mood to face anyone when I heard a hail from the dock behind me: "Hey, Bus." I paid no attention. A moment later I heard, "Hey, Bus." Again I paid no attention. At about the fourth hail, I turned with great annoyance to see Stanley standing there with a big grin on his face. "Here, catch," he said, tossing me a golf ball. The crew, I, and everyone around dissolved in laughter. He carried us through a very trying moment, for which I shall always be grateful. It did even more to show me how deeply he understood the objects in his camera lens. It is a pleasure to pay tribute publicly to a good and sensitive friend and great artist.

Emil "Bus" Mosbacher, Jr.
Skipper of America's Cup Yachts
Vim, Weatherly, and *Intrepid*
and Commodore of the New York
Yacht Club

A CENTURY UNDER SAIL

Introduction

When first researching material for this book, I came across an old negative preserver captioned in my father's strong hand, "Larchmont, July 27, 1913." That was the day I was born. The negative looked great—clear day, nice breeze. I wondered when the usual southwesterly breeze had come in that afternoon. As anyone might have guessed, Dad was away photographing the races off Larchmont. Neither my mother nor her children ever had any doubts about the priorities in my father's household.

I framed the box cover in which he stored this negative. Customarily, we filed negatives in their original boxes for handy retrieval. In this case the name of the plate manufacturer printed on the box was not "Eastman Extra Rapid" or "Wratten and Wainwright," but "Stanley," which must have been the inspiration for my name. The logo of this company showed a mounted horseman with the exhortation, "On, Stanley, On!"—a good motto to keep in mind. In particular it helped me with the task of selecting the photographs that appear in this book.

These two hundred or so images reflect the broad spectrum of yachting photography in the Rosenfeld Collection. The earliest negatives in our file date back to the 1880s, with three collections of glass plates from Aldridge, Bolles, and Burton, which my father, Morris Rosenfeld, acquired in about 1910. With more than a million images, the Rosenfeld file is the largest single collection of marine photographs in the world. It covers shipping, towboating, harbor craft, river craft, and most of the yachting history of the nation east of the Rockies. It includes America's Cup competition, ocean races, speedboat races, powerboats, steam yachts, and boatbuilding: a photographic chronicle of American yachting.

My father's devotion to yachting photography began at an early age. As a young teenager in lower Manhattan in the 1890s, he belonged to a camera club where he shared a camera with four other boys. With this borrowed camera, he roamed the crowded and noisy dockside along the East and Hudson rivers, fascinated by the horse-drawn wagons ashore and the steam and sail traffic afloat. In a shipyard on the East River near the Brooklyn Bridge, he photographed a three-masted ship with sails drying in the sun. This photograph won him a five-dollar prize in a photo contest, and with the five dollars he bought his own Gundlach camera from a pawnshop. In 1898, at the age of thirteen, he was already on his way to a career in photography.

After school and on summer vacations, he sought work in photography and studied art at Cooper Union on and off for a few years. Then in rapid strides he moved from managing a portrait studio on Fifth Avenue in New York in 1903, to freelancing from his house; then he moved into a rent-free office and darkroom loaned to him at the plant of the *Staats-Zeitung* newspaper. He did news photography for various papers and magazines, and covered society events and sports, particularly tennis, hunting, and sailing.

He went on all sorts of assignments. In those days, progress was taking place at such a rapid rate that a photographer had to be very aggressive. When his friend and competitor Jimmy Hare asked him to go along to North Carolina in 1903 to photograph two brothers who were going to try to fly an airplane, my father went to eight editors to get a twenty-dollar advance so he could cover the story. They told him he was wasting his time. As a result, he missed the first flight of the Wright Brothers.

When my father first came to photography in the early 1900s it was a time of new ideas, new things, new changes. The automobile, first a subject of some derision on muddy country roads, was roaring around racetracks at breakneck speed. Airplanes were tentatively taking to the air, and speedboats were churning across the water. In photography, new techniques and equipment were changing the nature of news reporting and giving the photographer a new prominence.

Even as early as the late 1880s, photographs were acquiring a new meaning in the publishing world. Whereas photographs had been used previously as an artist's reference for woodcuts which were printed on the presses, halftones made directly from photographs were beginning to appear in newspapers and magazines. The photographer was now a primary news source. With fast plates and shutters, he could capture the action of the day.

Coming to the photographic scene early in the history of action photography (and yachting photography, in particular), my father was able to take advantage of this new role of the photographer and join the small, very active group of news photographers, photojournalists, and photographic studios clustered around City Hall and nearby Newspaper Row.

By 1910, my father had his own studio on Nassau Street near Greeley Square in New York, and there was an increasing demand for his services, in both news and industrial photography. By 1920 his staff of eight was kept busy with daily assignments from a clientele that included AT&T, New York Telephone, Bell Telephone Labs, and Western Electric. One hundred and three index cards list assignments from AT&T in the years between 1910 and 1920. With fourteen lines to a card, they indicate that the studio was working on some photographic story for AT&T every other day during this ten-year period. By the late 1920s, my father had a staff of fourteen working on industrial, advertising, architectural, research, and news photography.

Although the expanding studio demanded much of my father's time, he always returned to his first love—marine photography. He covered speedboat and sailing races, particularly the America's Cup, which had a special attraction for him. He made every effort to photograph these races, regardless of the difficulties involved. In the beginning, he either had to hire a small boat as a photo chase boat or find some way to get aboard a committee or mark boat. Over the years he acquired his own chase boats, all appropriately named *Foto*. By 1930, in the fast and able 33-foot chase boat *Foto III,* it was possible to cover the America's Cup yachts through all the trials and races, as well as almost every other yachting event in the area. This was a time when we could recognize by name virtually every active yacht on the eastern seaboard between New York and Marblehead. Eventually, we had photographed most of them.

My father had a deep-rooted appreciation of the sea, an innate artistic eye, and a comprehensive knowledge of photography. If his camera, lens, or shutter was not right for an assignment, he experimented with a different combination. If his developer in the darkroom lacked contrast or detail when a new film or paper came along, he concocted a different chemical brew. All of this gave him an advantage in time, means, and talent that enabled him not just to take portraits of yachts like most previous marine photographers, but to interpret yachting from a consistent and aesthetic point of view. From the beginning, everyone remarked that Rosenfeld photographs were different.

That early summer of 1903 in a portrait studio was his first professional involvement with photography, and though he soon became a newsman, he never stopped searching for beauty or character in his subjects. He was very good at catching the significant moment and, just as important, being there when it happened. He blended the discipline of news-gathering with that of portraiture in a very comfortable way. The yachts in his photographs always looked their best, as it was against his nature to take an unflattering photograph of a boat.

While his knowledge of photography was extensive, when my father said he loved the sea, he meant in an intuitive way, without any particular knowledge or background in the sea or ships; he simply had a

Foto III, circa 1933

feeling for it. When afloat, he was always happy to have someone else handle the boat. In about 1905, he spent several months working with the studio of Edwin Levick on Fulton Street in New York and helped persuade him to buy a power launch as a photo boat. He offered to take it from the Hudson River to City Island by way of the Harlem and East rivers. On his first solo voyage he ran the boat hard aground on a rock near Hell Gate. He sat there, most uncomfortably, until the rising tide freed him. But the grounding did nothing to discourage his enthusiasm for boating, though in all the years we spent on photo chase boats, he almost never asked for the helm, much to the delight of his young sons. When not aiming a camera, he sat most contentedly on the stern seat, a white canvas hat on his head, a Havana cigar in his mouth, and a smile on his face.

In his youth, Morris Rosenfeld was aggressive and diligent. In his middle years he had an easy, outgoing social manner. When he entered a crowded room, voices hailed him and hands reached out toward him. Tall, dark-haired, with piercing green eyes, he had a commanding presence. I thought then, and still do, that he had some telepathic power. I learned very early that for me to match him "heads or tails" or "odds and evens" was a losing game.

Father was happy when his children were with him. There were four of us: the oldest, David, then myself, my sister Eleanor, and the youngest, William. He took a pixy pleasure in organizing us in work. We worked around the house, and we worked with him on the boat or in the studio or on location. The more of us, the merrier. Any childhood friend who came to visit was a legitimate target to be impressed or cajoled into a work detail. Most work, then, was really fun, and we enjoyed doing whatever he asked of us, so we couldn't complain. As we grew older and our business was more far-ranging, we began to work on our own, but he always liked to hear what we were doing and check up on us.

In 1927 we were living on City Island. *Foto I* was moored outside our window on Long Island Sound. The smell of sawdust and paint and the sounds of boatbuilding in the air characterized City Island, then a thriving yachting center. A virtual parade of yachts and shipping passed in front of our eyes. At the time, my father thought that City Island

was the most logical place for a marine photographer to bring up his family.

I was then fourteen and the island was a treasure trove. I fished, swam, rode, sailed, raced outboards, and went along with Dad. As my father had anticipated, we all loved the sea and photography, but he taught us nothing of either, at least directly. He did give us the chance to be on the water, to be near him, and to help him as he worked. He gave us no lessons in photography, but we had his example. He was a good companion, and if he was not a great teacher, he was a great competitor, with other photographers as well as with us. This was a trait I soon acquired. Though it helped the two of us through the years, it sometimes weighed on the rest of the family, as it did nothing to nurture camaraderie among the sons.

In March of 1933, during the depression that followed the stock market crash of 1929, President Franklin D. Roosevelt ordered all the banks in the United States closed. At the age of twenty, I reported for duty at the studio one day and found we did not have enough cash on hand to meet the payroll. My father was in Florida and only remotely concerned with the studio's situation. I was faced with the immediate prospect of laying off men, some of whom had been with us for a long time, most with families. This painful experience introduced me to the continuing struggle between the aesthetic and practical sides of studio life and of photography afloat. Fortunately the studio was able to thrive, and despite the depression, America's Cup racing continued with the years of the great J-class yachts.

The America's Cup races presented the marine photographer with some of the most interesting coverage possibilities afloat. As the country's premier yachting event, it brought together the most prominent names in yachting and the largest yachts. It was a gala social occasion as well as international news. The photographic files my father started in the studio became a historical document of America's Cup racing, and we all felt a personal and professional obligation to continue complete coverage of the event, an endeavor encouraged by the New York Yacht Club committees involved. I spent my first summer off Newport, Rhode Island, in *Foto III* on the America's Cup courses in 1930 and have photographed every Cup race since then.

During World War II I went into the navy, and Father ran the studio with the help of a staff that had been with us for a long time. After the war, we again had to build up a variety of compatible clients. I knew that to maintain a studio as a home base with darkroom facilities and staff required a broader spectrum of income-producing work than the yachting world alone offered. In 1948 we photographed sixty-seven steamships and tankers. The big ships helped provide the wherewithal for us to chase after small yachts. A supplemental income from sources besides yachting was almost always necessary to assure the financial health of the studio.

My father was in his sixties after the war, and we thought he might like to retire. In a few months this proved to be a poor idea, both for his health and for my mother's peace of mind, so he went back to work. He picked assignments that he thought he would enjoy, spent some inclement days at his desk in the studio, and, as long as he could travel with my mother, wintered in Florida. In the mid-1950s he suffered a few small strokes, and finally, one more serious. After my mother, Esther Rosenfeld, died in May 1962, my father lost much of his vigor and interest in the world. He died in 1968, at the age of eighty-three.

Morris Rosenfeld started a studio that has been in our family and continuously active since the turn of the century. For some years my two brothers were involved in it, but my brother David left in the 1930s to teach photography to high-school students in New York City, and my brother William left the studio in the 1960s to work for the National Association of Engine and Boat Manufacturers. My late wife, Ruth, a teacher and administrator for most of her life, joined me in the studio in the 1970s. We worked there together ashore; afloat, she took the helm of *Foto*. Unlike myself, my sons have not followed in their father's footsteps. Our son Richard is a computer programmer and teacher, and Jonathan is a psychiatrist. I, on the other hand, continue the tradition in marine photography, following yachting events in the United States and abroad, with particular attention to the America's Cup, maintaining the continuity of photographic files.

The studio has long had a life and identity of its own. Until the 1960s, all photographs taken by family and staff alike were credited to the studio name of Morris Rosenfeld. It was not until my father was quite ill that I began to think about establishing my own individual credit line. On December 12, 1984, the Rosenfeld Collection was acquired by Mystic Seaport Museum of Mystic, Connecticut. In those appropriate surroundings it will have a permanent home. A curatorial staff will nurture it and make it available to interested scholars, authors, yachtsmen, and collectors. Thus the Rosenfeld Collection will continue as a unique photographic resource.

Like my father, I have tried to be as realistic as possible in interpreting what my camera sees—with some license, of course, for the poetry in my soul. I have not used the most distorting lenses, the most violent contrasts, the most sensational angles. I have tried to show sailing as it is, admitting all along that I love the sea and almost every yacht afloat. If I do take a photograph and for some reason the boat doesn't look right, I discard the negative. This has been such a routine practice from my father's beginning in photography until today that I find it difficult to locate a negative in our files to illustrate the wrong way to photograph a yacht.

In other ways, however, my vision has differed to some extent from my father's. My photographs reflect more energy than my father's did. My temperament and training are different, and the cameras of today can more easily capture action and emotion. Also, the world and events proceed at a faster and more intense pace than in Dad's time, and recent photographs reflect this.

The studio, too, has evolved and changed with new developments in photographic equipment and techniques. From my father's first camera in 1898 to the present highly versatile, fast 35 mm cameras, photography has gone through many stages. My father used to recall making his own photographic emulsions and coating his own large-format glass plates at the turn of the century. In those days, change in photographic techniques came slowly to our studio. The old ways had their own charm and a great deal could be done with the old methods by an enterprising and aggressive photographer. The studio moved to new ways, but it always acknowledged its debt to the past. Most of the changes that occurred are reflected in our collection of nautical photographs. If the cameras have changed, the way they are used has changed just as dramatically.

In the 1870s, before the development of an instantaneous plate that was fast enough to allow exposures of a small fraction of a second, a photographer had to use a tripod to keep the camera still during the exposure time of a few seconds or more. Furthermore, everyone and everything had to remain still for those seconds in order to be recorded. The photographer could not stop action; he had to wait for the action to stop. If motion was not his concern, however, he could also make a two-minute exposure of a street scene, and the film would record in exact detail the cobblestones, buildings, lampposts, ashcans, and anyone taking a quiet siesta. What was not recorded and would not appear at all except as a "ghost image" were the people walking, strolling, and moving about, or the horses, carriages, and wagons coursing through the street. This is why we have so many "empty" street scenes taken at that time.

Instantaneous photographic plates were introduced in England in 1879 and came into use in the United States in the early 1880s. These fast plates revolutionized photography. They made action photography possible for the first time and opened new photographic vistas. Until that time, yachting photography had been virtually impossible.

By 1890 there were several yachting photographers active on the east coast of the United States. Among the best known were J. C. Hemment, J. S. Johnston, C. E. Bolles, and J. R. Burton of New York, and N. L. Stebbins of Boston. We owe most of our photographic records of the yachts of that time to them. They began in the discipline of landscape and portrait photography; most of their early negatives are, in fact, portraits of yachts.

Perhaps one of the earliest coffee-table books of yachting photographs was *American and English Yachts Illustrated,* published by Charles Scribner's Sons in 1887. It contains "A Treatise upon Yachts and Yachting" by the naval architect Edward Burgess. Burgess's treatise ran only fourteen pages, and N. L. Stebbins's fifty beautiful photogravure plates with captions were spread over one hundred pages. Although the name of Edward Burgess was printed four times larger than that of N. L. Stebbins on the title page, the book was a photographic achievement. All of the photographs were beautiful portraits of yachts surrounded by a large area of sky and water, in a landscape tradition.

This "portraiture" technique was the style of the times, a result of the kinds of equipment available. The relationship between the photographer and his camera on a physical and aesthetic level was very different then from what it is now. With a tripod-mounted camera, the photographer first selected a position for the tripod. In this decision-making process, the photographer established in his mind the image he sought on the photographic plate. The subject to be photographed and the relationship of objects within the frame of the picture were immutably selected the moment the tripod was set up.

When the camera was focused, the plate or film-holder inserted, the shutter set, and the holder slide drawn, the photographer, with shutter release cable in hand, could turn his attention again to the scene in front of him. At the right moment the exposure was made. Then the slide went back into the film-holder. If another photograph was desired, the camera had to be reloaded. Needless to say, this sequence of events precluded spontaneity.

Well into the 1930s, even in our own studio, some older photographers using an 8 × 10 tripod camera would look up just before exposing and with a winning smile say to anyone appearing in the photograph, "Still, please, still." The need for a subject to be still during an exposure was so imprinted on them that long after most of our staff were striving for natural expressions and body language, the old-timers, as their fingers touched the shutter release, would freeze their subjects with this outdated admonition.

When early yachting photographers went afloat, they carried over a tripod mentality because they had virtually no choice. At the proper distance from the yacht, they made their exposure. Because yachts of the day moved by at a relatively fast clip, the photographer could not hesitate.

Cameras were slow-working, and if the photographer was standing on an anchored vessel such as a committee boat or mark boat, his subject might be in shooting range for only a few seconds. This usually meant that a photographer had just one shot at his subject. He could seldom procure a moving launch or photo boat, which would have given him the ability to stay with his subject and be more selective. Almost all the early negatives in our collection were taken from a stationary boat or a dock. This began to change in 1920, when my father bought his first photo chase boat.

In the 1900s the reflex camera became a favorite of professional photographers. This was hand-held at about waist level; the photographer, by bending forward, looked down through an extended hood at the image shown on the ground glass. The reflex camera was more portable and afforded more immediacy than a tripod camera, but it had the great disadvantage in sports or news events of distancing the photographer from the subject. His body, partially off balance, was angled forward and down, his eyes were directed down into the camera, and all that faced the subject was the top of his head, or more likely the crown of his derby. The stance hardly encouraged intimacy between the photographer and his subject and could be positively dangerous on a rolling yacht.

George Eastman manufactured a daylight-loading roll-film camera in 1891, but the professionals clung stubbornly to their big reflex cameras for years afterward. By 1920 the Rosenfeld studio began to favor the Speed Graphic equipped with an eye-level finder. My father used 6½ × 8½-, 5 × 7-, and 4 × 5-inch formats. The Graphic gave the photographer a chance to be on his toes, to face the action in front of his camera, and to be more acutely aware of what was happening out there. It was particularly advantageous afloat on a small boat, where footing was difficult in almost all circumstances.

My father always preferred larger plates to smaller ones because he felt that with the emulsions available, a bigger plate size would make a better print. In fact, he was so convinced of this that although film emulsions became very fine-grained in his lifetime, he could never get himself to use a small 35 mm camera. He said it simply didn't feel right in his hands.

My father never objected to the weight of the large-format cameras he used; he often referred to the summer he spent as a boy hand-carrying block ice to the upper floors of apartment buildings, and the wonderful work it did for his arm and leg muscles. He was very proud that he had won his bicycle club's race from the Battery to Coney Island in 1902. The trophy he won may have been insignificant, but the exercise left a lasting mark on him, for even in his later years he had exceptionally good balance on legs that were still lithe and muscular.

For the younger members of our studio, such as my brothers and me, the 35 mm camera brought opportunities to be closer to the subjects we were photographing and to show people and body language as events occurred. Even though we went off in new directions with the 35 mm, the studio discipline of good printing and photographic excellence was always with us. It was a studio policy accepted and practiced by everyone. Not only did we have to find striking images, but we had to produce good prints as well.

My father and I did our first major story together using 35 mm cameras when we covered a regatta off Larchmont in 1939 for *Life* magazine. We shot the color section with Kodachrome, which had been introduced the year before. The vivid imagery of World War II, either directly to those who were in it or through photographic reporting in the news media, developed the fine reporting capabilities of the 35 mm camera. The camera's battery of lenses made it possible to photograph the subjects with an ease and intimacy previously unknown. Its small size, unobtrusiveness, and general acceptance made it possible to take close-ups without influencing the action being recorded.

For me, the 35 mm camera created opportunities to capture the energy, the motion, and the action at sea—the crew working on deck, the hull driving through seas, spray flying, and sails drawing—in a way that had not been possible with the more formal, bigger-format cameras. The 35 mm camera permitted an expression particularly suited to my own photographic philosophy in the postwar world.

In our studio, selecting the camera equipment and taking the actual photographs was often only a beginning. Many of our most creative moments occurred in the darkroom, where a photograph can be recomposed or almost remade. Emphasis, for example, can be directed to a particular area by changing the tonal values in the print. Often the sky printed directly from the negative is too light and the water too dark to interact harmoniously with the boat in a yachting photograph. However, with the negative projected on the easel, the photographer has in his hands the power to shade areas of the print and make them lighter, and to burn in areas and make them darker. Each such change redirects the eye within the image. If the highlight along the luff of the sail is burned in a little, the fabric shows more tone and texture and the lines of the sail panels add interesting curves to give roundness and form. The print can be improved again, and if patience and time permit, the process can be repeated. Every enlargement made in the Rosenfeld studio was to some degree, and sometimes to a very large degree, shaped and formed by the person printing it.

In the early days, improving images was difficult. The negative material then was orthochromatic, sensitive to blue light almost without distinction to the blue of the sky and the white of the clouds. In the early 1900s, photographs with dark skies and brilliant clouds, which we expect today, were very unusual, and over the years we have used diverse ways to enhance the plainness of the skies in old negatives. When I was young and spending time after school in the studio, I would often be given a package of prints with instructions to take them to Mr. Fried for clouds. Fried was an accomplished airbrusher who created clouds on demand, from just a wisp of cloud to colossal cumulus clouds. My instructions were to have Mr. Fried put twenty-five cents' worth of clouds in one print where just a suggestion was needed, fifty cents' worth of clouds where an overall pattern was called for, and a dollar's worth if a major cloud operation was in order. I watched with great satisfaction while the clouds grew just where we wanted them.

After Eastman panchromatic film came on the market in 1913, we photographed a library of clouds. We had cumulus clouds, cumulonimbus clouds, mare's-tails, thunderheads—an entire repertoire of clouds that could be double-printed as images where nature had provided none at the time. We would put the negative showing the boat in one enlarger and the cloud negative we meant to double-print in another. After sketching the outline of the boat on a blank piece of paper, we moved it to the enlarger loaded with the clouds and placed them appropriately around the boat.

We would then print the negative, shading the sky with our hands, dodging the water and hull, burning in and shading the sails where necessary. After moving the easel to the cloud-equipped enlarger, we would print the clouds, being careful to shade with our hands all of the area of the paper previously printed. This was painstaking and without scientific controls. We really felt our way, and very seldom were we satisfied with the first few prints.

Double-printing clouds was an exercise we approached rather carefully, for it was time-consuming and tied up a darkroom, often with a printer, developer, and assistant, for hours. It is no secret that some of our prints wear clouds that never flew over the yachts beneath them. Some of them may actually have floated through skies many miles distant and decades away in time, but they seem right to us, and we have never known a yacht to complain.

When I print an old negative, as with some of the images in this book, I often find myself in conflict. With the old negative projected on the printing easel, I am tempted to print the sky area with darker tones than were ever there before. Having become accustomed to the strong skies that filtered panchromatic film provides on a clear day, I must exert an effort of will to print an old negative the way it was printed at the turn of the century. Also, I often want to enlarge just a section of the negative, rather than print the entire negative the way it was made. Our new battery of lenses has made it possible for me to move closer to the action for the last forty years, so that returning to the more formal past takes considerable readjustment. Film, cameras, and lenses are not the only determinants involved in the changes in marine photography during this century; attitudes and philosophies also exert a powerful influence on the resulting image.

While new cameras and developing techniques gave us flexibility on a shoot and in the darkroom, our photo chase boat provided a mobility that completely changed the nature of our photography. In order to get out on the water near the racing fleet, my father acquired *Foto I* in 1920, our first photo chase boat. We had four *Foto*s over the years. The first, a 32-foot Red Bank dory-type, one of a group originally built for the police department in New York, was able and very comfortable, but at 10 knots proved much too slow for the big schooners sailing in the 1920s.

Foto II, a 26-foot Hacker runabout, was very fast, but for a photographer who often had to be out there when the seas were big and the spray was flying, she was bouncy and wet. My father went into conference with Frederick K. Lord, a designer of fast speedboats and comfortable commuter boats, in an effort to come up with the perfect photo chase boat. As a result, in 1929 we went out on the water in a 33-foot V-bottom hunter-cabin power launch which was close to ideal for the next fifty years.

Foto III was fast, fast enough to catch up with just about every yacht we chased, and fast enough to make a day trip from Marblehead to City Island or to run back from Block Island after covering the start of a Bermuda Race. Speed gave us the opportunity to really cover the cruising fleet as well as a race around the buoys. It allowed us to linger at a mark of the course and then run ahead to the next probable point of action. We had no more frustrating incidents caused by big yachts sailing away from us. *Foto III* was more than fast. She accelerated rapidly and turned sharply. We had a photo platform that could be moved quickly and maneuvered rapidly to get us where we wanted to be, and if we got into a tight spot, *Foto III* got us out of trouble fast.

Fred Lord had designed a rather classic boat, and since *Foto III* was out on the water all summer, her long, lean lines became familiar to yachtsmen along the east coast from New York to Marblehead. Because *Foto* came close to the racing fleet but never interfered, we gained an acceptance that gave us the option to get even closer to the action. It was not at all uncommon when we approached a committee boat to hear someone aboard say, "Well, Rosie's here—we can start now."

Most yachtsmen assumed from the name *Foto* that we had a darkroom and processing facilities aboard. Actually, we had neither. On many an evening we did cover the portlights to darken the cabin so that we could reload the film and plateholders we had aboard, but that was the extent of our need for floating darkroom facilities. The processing of film was a very careful procedure reserved for the studio in Manhattan or for the darkroom in the basement of our home on City Island.

A few little idiosyncrasies in *Foto*'s behavior, while not diminishing our belief that she was an ideal photo chase boat, gave us some moments that ranged from distraction to despair. Because the hull was V-bottomed and narrow, it had a sharp roll. Roll is hardly the proper description—*Foto III* had a severe snap in a heavy beam sea. This motion could be considered a virtue since it brought us back to even keel very quickly, but on rare occasions, cameras flew up and off their perch on the engine hatch, and if those aboard weren't quick in their nautical two-step, they too would take off. This was a condition one learned to live with by either anticipating the big seas or nursing the boat over them.

I acquired my first fiberglass boat, *Foto IV*, in 1978. I felt the need to go faster and to cover greater distances. *Foto IV*, powered with twin engines, could make 30 knots and cruise comfortably at 20. Although some years I both steered the boat and worked the cameras, I found it ideal to have an experienced person at the helm.

The helmsman's skill is most important. In the heat of the chase, the interplay between the helmsman and the photographer provides a sometimes unbelievable backdrop to a day's shoot. Usually friends or family have been at the helm aboard *Foto*, but over the years many hundreds of people in various parts of the world have taken the helm while I have been behind the cameras.

Although the tension implicit in the act of working the camera is sometimes easily forgotten by the experienced photographer, it is never forgotten by the helmsman. I thought after many years of hearing and barking such commands as "Back her ahead!," "Closer away!," and "Left-right-left!," I had developed into a perfect communicator. Evidently this is not yet true.

During the 1983 America's Cup races so winningly sailed by *Australia II*, I needed a larger boat than *Foto IV* as a chase boat. Charlie Dana was kind enough to offer his splendid *St. Roque,* and spelled by his wife, Posy, he took the helm all through the series. After the last race Dana remarked, "It was fun steering for you the past two weeks—or was it the past two years?" As we parted he presented me with a book written by Richard Henry Dana, one of his illustrious forebears. It was, of course, *Two Years Before the Mast.*

In all the miles we logged on the four *Fotos,* no accident marred the rapport we had with the boats. They all took to the water serenely, with just one exception. *Foto II,* moored in front of the house in City Island, broke loose during the night in a hurricane in 1929 and washed up on the rocks along the shore, damaged beyond repair.

Only once in all the years I have been afloat has a boat sunk under me. In 1980, while covering the arrival of the OSTAR fleet with a group of photographers in a chartered 40-foot sportfisherman, we powered past Block Island to meet a French arrival. We rode an easy six-foot swell in a haze that limited visibility to half a mile. Going over a swell, the boat hesitated before righting itself. I called the captain down, and when he went below, he lifted the hatch in the cabin sole to find water gushing up through the bottom. In two and a half minutes, all but a few feet of the bow was under water.

As the boat settled, I walked forward to find that the only other person aboard was the captain's young wife, who was obviously very nervous. Anxious to take her mind off the situation, I smiled at her and asked in a conversational tone, "Is this your first sinking?" She replied, "Why, yes—is it yours too?" I said it was, and we started chatting as the water slowly rose over our ankles.

We were interrupted by her husband, who was shouting to her to jump overboard immediately and swim away from the boat. She did, and I joined her shortly. Fortunately, the captain had had the foresight to bring aboard his own flares, one of which caught the eye of the only vessel on the horizon. We were all rescued twenty minutes later by a charming skipper who enthusiastically greeted each of us as we were hauled over the side with, "My name is Robert E. Lee, same as the general! Welcome aboard!"

With our *Fotos* we ranged the coast summer after summer, photographing the yachting scene. In the course of time, we accumulated a comprehensive file of yachts and yachtsmen, of ocean rcaces and round-the-buoy regattas. Day by day, *Foto* provided many rewards far beyond her primary mission. For one thing, voyaging aboard *Foto* made us weather-wise: we were out in fog and calm and wind and rain. We learned what a weather front would bring, off what points the waves were strongest, and where the currents ran fast.

As I learned more about the weather and the waters, I learned the ways of boats in them. I knew how different boats rose with one wave and settled into the next, how water was tossed off the deck, how spray flew out and up, how sails breathed and slatted, how headstays sagged. I learned how sunlight could give a sail fullness, form, and texture, or take all shape and feel away.

I knew that a quiet, cloudless easterly was a poor photographic day, no matter how brightly the sun was shining. If a fast-moving front brought in a boisterous westerly, it was good to shoot early before the cloud cover built up. On a run from the Race to Block Island on a foggy day before radar, if the southerly swell moved abaft our beam, I could tell I was getting under the lee and was close inshore.

Men have had love affairs with their boats since the beginning of nautical history. Long ago, I thought I understood boats and boating, but only recently have I begun to realize just how much a boat can give. Somewhere in the photographs in this book, to some little or large extent, each understanding we gained of the ways of water and boats is reflected. We show many moods of weather and sailors, the power of wind and waves, and the play of light and shadow on sail and sea.

Of course the photographs have their own story to tell. The camera is an unusual instrument. It looks both ways—through the eye of the photographer into his subject, and into the mind of the photographer through the subject he captures. Thus, while these photographs illustrate one hundred years of yachting history, they also reveal the story of the Rosenfelds afloat.

PART ONE

Gaff-Riggers and Schooners
1884–1929

*I*t was a time of controversy in America's Cup racing—argument about the development of new designs, the use of new and exotic materials in boatbuilding, masts getting taller, and sails getting larger. Small craft were racing for speed, and new, large, one-design classes were being built. Cargo schooners tried to make a go under sail, while other sailing yachts strove for transatlantic records. While all of the above could be said about the present day, the time I am describing is the turn of the century, the years before and after 1900.

Yachtsmen of the era thought big. In 1906 the New York Yacht Club Squadron enrolled 324 steam- or auxiliary-powered yachts longer than 100 feet overall, more than ever again. In 1903 the America's Cup defender *Reliance* set 16,160 square feet of sail for a record in sail area.

In the eighteen years between 1885 and 1903, eight America's Cup races took place. This was more than in any other eighteen-year period since the Cup was won by the yacht *America* in 1851. The original *America* was still sailing, her schooner rig in marked contrast to the magnificent gaff-riggers then racing. Public interest in the races was widespread and partisan. Cartoonists had a field day in the press, scoffing at the conditions of the race, the contenders, and the nations represented. Then as now, controversy was integral to the America's Cup. In the Lord Dunraven challenge of 1885, early bickering developed into a big fracas with the newspapers printing charges of "fraud" and "infamous slander." On the other hand, Sir Thomas Lipton's challenge in 1899 opened an era of goodwill and good sportsmanship in America's Cup competition.

Although America's Cup racing was a yachting event apart and special, competition between the magnificent schooners sailing early in the century was frequent, both for sport and for money. Often the larger the yacht, the higher the wager. In 1899 over a course around Block Island, three schooners raced for a $1,000 prize. When the big yachts were not racing for prizes, they were trying to set records. The three-masted schooner yacht *Atlantic* set a transatlantic speed record in 1905 that stood until 1980. Small boats also engaged in lively competition. In New York Bay, 15-foot sandbaggers with big-footed jibs set on bowsprits longer than the boat itself and huge mainsails also raced for sport and gain.

All through the first few decades of the 1900s, a few full-rigged ships and many working and fishing schooners sailed off the east coast. The old schooners sometimes had patched sails and rust-scarred hulls, which on a yacht would have indicated neglect but on the working schooners seemed a mellowing to be respected and appreciated. Sometimes the crews of the fishing schooners would take a few days off to go racing, and it would become an international event that for fishing schooner buffs more than equaled America's Cup racing.

Long-distance ocean racing also became popular at this time. In 1905 Thomas Fleming Day, then editor of *Rudder* magazine, needled his readers by writing that though they often talked about the seagoing qualities of their yachts, they seldom sailed far from the sight of land. To meet his challenge, three small yachts sailed a race from Gravesend Bay, New York, to Bermuda in 1906. The Bermuda Race has become the east coast's most classic ocean race. In this section a photograph shows the crew of *Micco,* one of the contestants in 1924.

Along with spirited racing, the period was also marked by innovations in yacht design. As early as 1880, a design battle began between narrow, deep-keel cutters and wide, shallow, centerboard sloops. The cutters traditionally followed English lines and were essentially more seaworthy and suited to the deep, rough waters surrounding the British Isles. American sloops were suited to protected coastal waters and the shallow bays of New England and New York. A compromise design developed that was wider than the cutter and deeper than the sloops.

For the America's Cup race in 1895 Nathanael Herreshoff designed *Defender,* using manganese-bronze hull plating with aluminum topsides. In 1913 the prolific Herreshoff designed and built the largest one-design yachts in history. This new cruising/racing class, the New York Yacht Club 50s, were 50 feet on the waterline and 72 feet on deck.

Of course cameras and photographic techniques were changing too, although as new ways were introduced, old ways lingered. At the turn of the century, my father still occasionally made photographic emulsions and coated large-format glass plates, although manufactured ones were available. Most professional photographers moved slowly from large-format cameras to smaller ones. With one exception, all the photographs here that were taken before 1907 were on 8 × 10-inch glass plates. My father still carried an 8 × 10 camera at the 1920 America's Cup races, although from 1910 on he favored a 6½ × 8½ format. Through the 1920s the 5 × 7 Graphic, the camera I first used, was our studio's standard equipment on location afloat. Cameras over the decades were getting smaller, and films were becoming more versatile.

At the turn of the century my father was working on Newspaper Row in Manhattan and the interest and excitement of the press in America's Cup racing nurtured his own innate interest in yachts and yachting. By the time *Resolute* and *Vanitie* were racing in the next decade, his interest had developed into a passion that motivated the studio from then on.

The photographs here reflect this dedication to the America's Cup races and highlight other events in the yachting scene at the time. Not only do they illustrate a history of changing yachts and crews, they also show how even the surface of the sea changes with time.

Athlon, 1884

Athlon was a compromise sloop built in 1884. Sloops of the time were normally wide and shallow, while cutters were narrow and deep. Built to measurements "in between," *Athlon* had hull design features characteristic of both types. In addition, she had a double headrig with a forestaysail and jib instead of the huge single jibs on most sloops.

The Sandbagger, 1893

Speed under sail was coveted in the 1880s and 1890s by small yachts as well as large. The sandbaggers were centerboard hulls, usually about 15 feet long with enormous rigs. Their ballast included a 50-pound sandbag for each crewman. The sandbags were shifted to the weather rail after each tack, and if the wind piped up, the crew followed. Here a little sandbagger bowls along with a bone in her teeth, though the gentle breeze hardly ripples the water.

The original, an 8 × 10 glass plate, is in beautiful focus. The seams in the old canvas sails are vertical and show clearly in this photograph. Multispeed shutters were developed about this time, permitting shutter speeds of over 1/500 second.

Iroquois, 1886

Built in 1886, *Iroquois,* a steel schooner measuring 98 feet overall, reflected the trend in design toward a more seaworthy form and stronger construction. On March 12, 1888, the great blizzard of that year struck the West Indies–bound *Iroquois.* She survived the gale, but an older, 100-foot yacht, *Cythera,* was lost with all hands.

Emerald, 1893

Big schooners were the cream of the cruising racing fleets in the 1880s and the 1890s. Twelve of them crossed the starting line of the Commodore's Cup Race in August of 1893. *Emerald,* 112 feet overall, was the newest addition to the fleet.

America, 1893

After the yacht *America* won the coveted America's Cup in 1851, she had a long career that included a stint as a blockade-runner during the Civil War. Scuttled to keep her from being captured, she was found on the bottom, upriver from Jacksonville, Florida. She was sold by the navy in 1873 to Brigadier General B. F. Butler. The general was a colorful character, a soldier, politician, governor of Massachusetts, and presidential candidate. The general, his son, or a grandson raced *America* almost every summer until 1901, and she won races through 1897. In 1887 the sleek black hull was rebuilt, rerigged, and painted white. She is sailing here in her new rig and her new paint about 1893.

Cup Yachts Hauled Out in Erie Basin, 1893

In 1893, four new potential America's Cup defenders were built. Two of them are hauled out in Erie Basin, Brooklyn— a common sight that summer. Because the hulls were built of steel and rusted quickly, the yachts had to be hauled frequently so that the rough scale could be polished to a suitable racing bottom. *Jubilee,* on the left, was designed by John B. Paine; *Colonia,* on the right, was designed and built by Herreshoff. Neither proved the equal of *Vigilant,* the successful defender. In the background, the yards and rigging of the sailing ships that still plied the waters of New York stand in marked contrast to the big sloops in the foreground.

The negative from which this print was made, one of the originals in our file, is an instantaneous quarter plate, $3\frac{1}{4} \times 4\frac{1}{4}$ inches. This size had become popular with amateur photographers using hand-held cameras in the previous decade. The lens was wide open to get stop-action exposure on what seems to be a gray day. If it had been brighter and the photographer could have stopped down his lens, the print might have been sharp all the way across. As it is, the edges run out of focus.

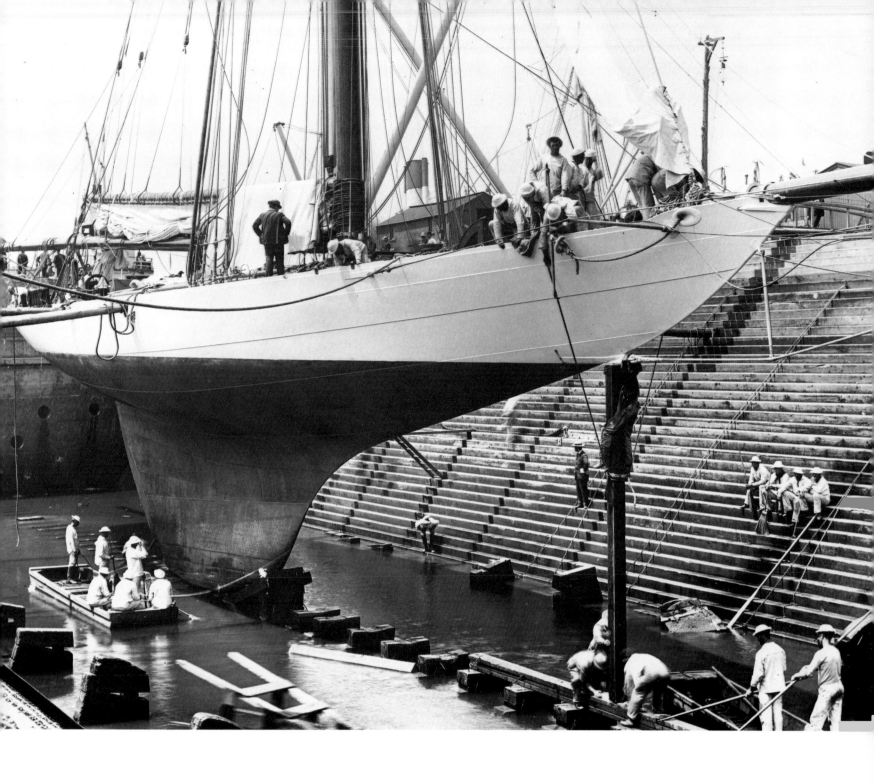

Defender in Dry Dock, 1895

At 123 feet on deck and 88 feet on the waterline, *Defender,* the keel cutter designed and built by Herreshoff, defeated *Valkyrie III* in the America's Cup race of 1895. In Erie Basin the water has just been pumped out of the drydock so that it is level with the foot of the keel. The crew, in the scow alongside and sitting on the steps of the dock, have brooms in hand

ready to give the bottom the customary cleaning and scraping, made easier by the manganese bronze used in the bottom plating.

The negative is an 8 × 10-inch glass plate taken with a view camera that has been carefully focused so that all areas are sharp. The lens was obviously stopped down, and the exposure must have been

a second or two. A crewman descending the steps near the center of the picture and the heads of the men at the foot of the bow are blurred because they have moved during the exposure time. The photographer, with the skill acquired in watching for moving figures, has managed to catch a moment when everyone else in view was standing relatively still.

Hoisting the Mainsail Aboard *Defender*,
1895

All hands are on the main halyards, to
both port and starboard, aboard the big
gaff-rigged sloop *Defender* in 1895. At
the wheel is Captain Hank Haff, one of
the famous professional skippers who
sailed these boats.

The original, an 8 × 10 glass plate, was
probably made with a hand-held camera.
The lens was short-focus so it could take

in the area covered on the deck. Most
professional photographers had several
lenses of different focal lengths with tripod-mounted cameras, but only the more
mechanically inclined had a variety of
lenses with hand-held cameras, as a different set of lens stops and focus scales
was required for each lens.

Defender Under Spinnaker, 1895

Each new Herreshoff-designed defender during the 1890s carried more sail area than the one before. *Defender,* in 1895, set 13,500 square feet of sail, a seemingly astronomical figure for the times, but the challenger *Valkyrie III* set 400 feet more. Here *Defender* flies a spinnaker, balloon jib, jib, mainsail, and club topsail. Underneath the bowsprit in the stern of the stake boat a photographer stands, legs wide apart for balance, a big 8 × 10 reflex camera in his hands. The original negative is an 8 × 10 glass plate.

Columbia and *Shamrock*, 1899

On an unusually sunny afternoon in the October 1899 America's Cup series, all hands scramble to set spinnakers as *Columbia* leads *Shamrock* on a 15-mile run to the finish line at the Sandy Hook lightship. October was chosen for the series as the most likely time to find favorable racing weather off New York harbor. This October was contrary. Fog and calm prevailed, and it required thirteen tries before three races were sailed, all won by *Columbia*. This was the first news event to be transmitted by "the Marconi system of wireless telegraphy" from the scene to newspaper offices, in this case, 40 miles away. The *Herald* was pleased to report that "mist baffled land observers and signal balloons and carrier pigeons alike failed." The original is an 8 × 10 glass plate.

26

Nathanael Herreshoff

Nathanael Herreshoff, 1848–1934, legendary designer and builder of five America's Cup defenders between 1893 and 1920, had no equal during his lifetime.

Shamrock and Erin, 1899

The first of the succession of five *Sham-rock*s that Sir Thomas Lipton, the tea baron, sent over for the America's Cup between 1899 and 1930 is sailing with sheets started past Sir Thomas's 287-foot steam yacht *Erin*. The topmast aboard *Shamrock* towered 132 feet over the deck, a height made more vivid by comparison with the figure of the topmast man comfortably seated aloft on the big spreader.

The original is an 8 × 10 glass plate. Taken on a day with smooth water and clear atmosphere, the negative is as crisp as the weather; each line of the rigging stands out against the sky.

Shamrock and Columbia, 1899

In a close start, *Shamrock* and *Columbia* provide the photographer with a moment of keen competitive racing. Despite some exciting moments during the series, *Shamrock* lost to *Columbia* in three straight races. On the night of the last race, Sir Thomas sent word to the New York Yacht Club that he would challenge again, and he returned in 1901.

These moments of action were rare treats for the photographer of the day. Bound to a stationary location, in this case the committee boat, he could usually photograph little of the race. If the action didn't happen in front of him at the start or finish, it might just as well not happen at all. On the other hand, if it happened in sight but out of camera range, it caused the photographer a pain that was usually not assuaged until he arrived at a bar ashore.

Constitution and *Columbia*, 1901

Constitution and *Columbia* (in the foreground) glide under curved spinnakers in an early Cup trial. At the beginning of the 1901 season, three 90-footers, *Constitution*, *Columbia*, and *Independence*, were tuning up for the America's Cup elimination trials. All were about 90 feet on the waterline and over 130 feet on deck, and each set over 13,000 square feet of canvas. *Independence* soon withdrew. Between July and September 5, *Constitution* and *Columbia* raced eighteen times. *Columbia* won exactly half of the races but was selected to be the defender "by virtue of overall performance."

Shamrock II and *Columbia*, 1901

Shamrock II, on the left, and *Columbia* are jockeying for position before the start of a race in the 1901 series. Judging from the way the crews are seated, each vessel has been on its tack for some time. These big boats at the turn of the century had their close moments similar to today's 12-meters, though they occurred at a slower pace. On the wind, the old gaff-riggers were a pattern of angles.

Reliance, 1903

Reliance successfully defended the America's Cup against *Shamrock III* in 1903. A big, 143-foot overall, scow-type craft, *Reliance* set 16,160 square feet of sail, the most sail set by any contestant in the America's Cup races. The weather was kind to *Reliance* all during the series. The wind was light and *Reliance* was able to use all her sails through all the races. *Shamrock III* had a beautifully finished hull but *Reliance,* with her giant sail power, won each race.

The original is an 8 × 10 glass plate and is, like most of the reflex camera images of the time, horizontal in format. The image of *Reliance* was greatly enlarged and printed vertically to suggest the height and power of the sails.

Bowsprit *Reliance,* 1903

At least eighteen of the crew of big *Reliance* are out along the bowsprit as the jib topsail is lowered.

This print represents an area that in the original 8 × 10 negative could easily be hidden by a fingernail. The old negatives of racing scenes were taken from a distance, and almost all of the ones in our file show the entire yacht. The few close-up detail shots that show men working were taken from on board. Since few, if any, of the old-time photographers had photo chase boats to work from, they were seldom close to the action. I would like to think that if we had been there with *Foto,* we would somehow have managed to get under the bowsprit to show details of the clawing hands and gripping toes as they hung on and manhandled the sail. This enlargement of a little section of the negative shows the spirit of the action despite the grain in the print.

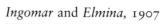
Ingomar and *Elmina,* 1907

Schooners had been racing for big stakes from the time yacht racing began in America—sometime around 1850. *Ingomar* and *Elmina,* on the right, were both 87 feet on the waterline and about 126 feet on deck. Both schooners have just come about and are sheeting in on a new tack. The masthead man is working with the foretopsail still clewed up as it was in tacking.

This 8 × 10 glass plate is one of the best early examples of the quality and detail that pyro developer gave to these negatives. The photograph was taken against the light but includes great detail in both the shadow area of the sails and the highlights on the water. The shutter speed, probably 1/500 second, is fast enough to stop the action of the boats without freezing the flying spray.

Resolute, 1914

Three 75-footers were built for the America's Cup series planned for 1914. The third, *Defiance,* was eliminated early. The trials took place between *Resolute* and *Vanitie,* who were to continue to be rivals for years afterward, even after they were schooner-rigged. World War I caused postponement until 1920, which was the last America's Cup race with these traditional gaff rigs and huge topsails. The modern jib-headed or marconi rig came into use with the J-boats of 1930.

The negative is an 8 × 10 glass plate taken with a multispeed between-the-lens shutter.

Vanitie, 1914

Vanitie was built for the America's Cup challenge planned for 1914. She was designed by the versatile William Gardner of Boston, who also designed the graceful three-masted schooner *Atlantic* as well as the internationally raced Star class.

This 8 × 10 glass plate has an unusual quality for its time. My father took this photograph directly into the sunlight, but the original negative was processed so carefully that the tone of the photograph is preserved and the clouds appear clearly, something almost never seen in early orthochromatic film. Introduced in 1913, this plate is a Wratten and Wainwright panchromatic emulsion, which was more sensitive to the entire range of light in the spectrum. The print has been worked to enhance the tones.

NYYC 50s, 1913

In 1913 Nathanael Herreshoff designed and built nine one-design sloops 72 feet on deck and 50 feet on the waterline. The New York Yacht Club 50s were the largest class of one-design yachts of this size in the history of yachting. Their rigging was simple: a big single jib on a club, a small jib, and a topsail set above. They were meant to be sailed by a small professional crew consisting of a captain, two sailors, and a steward. Complete with sails, they cost only $17,000, an unbeliev-

able price in today's market. After a few years of lively competition, changing times and styles after World War I inhibited NYYC 50 class racing, but some of this class still sail today, though under different rigs.

The negative is a 6½ × 8½ glass plate, my father's favorite format between 1910 and 1925. From the camera angle it would seem this photograph is one of the first to be taken from a photo chase boat.

K Class, 1907

In 1907, the three 85-footers *Istalena, Winsome,* and *Aurora* frequently raced together off Oyster Bay and Glen Cove on Long Island Sound. All three were designed and built by Herreshoff and were the only yachts in the class. Here one of them sails off Oyster Bay in a rail-down, southeasterly breeze.

Start, 1920 America's Cup, *Resolute* and *Shamrock IV*

In 1920, for the first time in America's Cup racing, amateurs skippered the boats. William (later Sir William) Burton captained *Shamrock IV*, right, and Charles Francis Adams led *Resolute*, left. Also for the first time, Sir Thomas Lipton saw one of his *Shamrock*s win a race. *Shamrock IV* actually won two straight races of the three needed for victory. The first was won when a sail-trimming error caused *Resolute* to lose a halyard and the mainsail was dropped. *Resolute* withdrew. During the second race, *Shamrock IV* won the start, as shown, then found the right breeze at the right time and, with the cheers of the spectators and the horns of the fleet sounding, sailed across the finish line ten minutes ahead of *Resolute*. Unfortunately for Sir Thomas, *Resolute* won the next three in a row. The print is from an 8 × 10 glass plate.

Shamrock IV Deck View, 1920

Shamrock IV sailed to the United States in 1914 and was crossing the Atlantic when World War I broke out. She was laid up in New York and recommissioned when the America's Cup series started again in 1920. This deck view was taken in June of 1920 as *Shamrock IV* sailed by Sir Thomas Lipton's yacht *Erin* during early tuning trials. The negative was made with a 5 × 7 Graphic. It probably shows the most detail on deck of any action photograph of that period.

Aboard *Erin*, 1920

On the deck of his steam yacht *Erin*, surrounded by cheerful guests, Sir Thomas Lipton hardly looks like a man watching his fourth multimillion-dollar challenge for the America's Cup slip away. From his first try in 1899 to his last in 1930, Sir Thomas challenged for the Cup five times. He became as famous for his good sportsmanship as for his tenacity. Second and third from the right are Rose and Joseph Kennedy. Forty-two years later their son, President John F. Kennedy, watched a race in the 1962 Cup series off Newport from the deck of a navy destroyer, the U.S.S. *Joseph P. Kennedy, Jr.*

The negative is a 5 × 7 glass plate taken with a Graphlex camera. Judging from the happy faces, it is very possible that my father's cigar had just bounced off the corner of the camera's big hood. In those days, a cigar was almost always in Dad's mouth and sometimes pressed into service as a device to put subjects at ease.

The Highball Express, 1920

Here a yachting party observes the America's Cup races of 1920 from an unusual addition to the spectator fleet. This Curtiss 5FL, converted by Aeromarine (a company founded by the yachtsman Ingalls Uppercu), ran between New York and Key West in the winters of the early 1920s with stops in Atlantic City; Beaufort, South Carolina; and Miami, Florida. Known as the Highball Express, it also brought its well-to-do passengers to Cuba during Prohibition.

Gloucester Fishing Schooner, 1938

The Gloucester fishing schooners were fast and able, built to make quick trips from the fishing banks to the markets whether the wind was fair or foul. The schooners raced against each other several times off Gloucester, Massachusetts. Often the subject of some lively betting, the fishing vessels had loyal partisans. *Gertrude L. Thebaud* appears above, and on the facing page *Thebaud* leads *Bluenose*, the winner of the International Fishermen's Races of 1922.

Gloucester Fishermen, 1923

In the 1923 Fishermen's Races, the *Elizabeth Ann Howard* is seen from the deck of the *Henry Ford* as the two approach the finish line against the late afternoon sun.

Deck of *Henry Ford*, 1923

In the Fishermen's Races of 1923, the Gloucester fishing schooner *Henry Ford* took a knockdown. My father was aboard. As the deck heeled sharply, his leather camera bag with another camera and all of his exposed film started sliding down the deck toward the rushing water.

A sailor jumped past him to save the bag; his shoulder appears as a dark mass in the lower left corner of the print. Both this photograph and the preceding one were made on 5 × 7 glass plates with a Graphic camera fitted with a wide-angle lens.

Working schooners sailing along the eastern seaboard were a welcome sight all through the early 1900s. Because of the canny and economical way they were maintained and sailed, they held on despite the competition from steamboats, railroads, diesel freighters, and heavy trucks. Often scarred, rusted, and patched, they were always a delight to the eye. On the facing page, the four-masted *Cumberland Queen*, deeply laden, sails in the calm waters of Block Island Sound. To the right above, vessels at anchor off City Island, New York, await the tide and a fair wind to sail eastward. Below, the *H. S. Whiton*, with sheets started, bowls along under ideal conditions — a fair wind and smooth sea. The photographs of the coasters span three decades. My father photographed the *Whiton* at the turn of the century, the *Cumberland Queen* in 1921, and the anchored fleet in the late 1920s.

The *Cumberland Queen* is on a 6½ × 8½ glass plate. The anchored fleet is on 5 × 7 panchromatic film. This kind of photograph might pass for a moonlight scene, but it was taken at high noon. The negative of the *Whiton* was photographed on an 8 × 10 glass plate in 1902.

Tusitala, 1925

Above, the full-rigged ship *Tusitala* (sailed by the Farrell Lines) is returning to the port of New York laden with cargo from Africa. As the air is light, a tug waiting offshore will rendezvous with *Tusitala* and tow her to the dock. These cargo ships had only wind for power. To the right, though there is not enough wind to fill the ship's sails, a heavy swell is rolling in toward shore. *Tusitala* dips behind the sea which rises higher than her decks. Both photographs are on 5 × 7 glass plates, taken with a Graphic camera and exposed with a focal-plane shutter.

Tusitala Under Tow, 1925

The full-rigged ship *Tusitala,* returning laden with cargo from across the South Atlantic, has run out of wind approaching the port of New York. The steam tug *Federal No. 1* tows *Tusitala* under a billowing cloud of black smoke, while another tug can be seen alongside to starboard. The second tug will assist *Federal No. 1* in maneuvering *Tusitala* alongside the dock. The photograph was taken on a 5 × 7 glass plate with a Graphic camera and was exposed with a focal-plane shutter.

Crew of *Micco* and Bermuda Racer
Micco, 1924

In 1924 the centerboard ketch *Micco*, 40 feet, 6 inches at the waterline, shown on the facing page in light airs at the start, was one of the contestants. Above, her crew relaxes on the morning of the race. They present an informative study of the yachting fashions of that year. From left to right, the ultimate in natural footgear, then a more sophisticated version of yachting apparel, shoes topped by plus fours, a well-knotted tie, and a jaunty driving cap. Behind him is a genuine sailor suit, and next to him is an example of standout collegiate fashion with saddle oxfords. Following, we have a paint-stained jogging outfit of the day. Finally, the urban version of the yachtsman in his fedora and pin-striped suit completes the picture. The Bermuda Race, a four- to six-day excursion often in heavy seas and bad weather, was all fun in those days. The original negatives are 5 × 7 glass plates taken with a Graphic camera and a focal-plane shutter.

Atlantic, 1929

Atlantic, a 185-foot, three-masted schooner designed by William Gardner in 1903, was an outstanding yacht and a popular favorite for decades. In the Kaiser's Cup Race of 1905, *Atlantic* set a record sailing from New York to England in twelve days and fourteen hours, unmatched until Eric Tabarly bettered it in 1980.

In September of 1929, *Atlantic*'s owner cabled us to come out and meet him down the Sound for a photographic session. It was one of those rare days when the right yacht was sailing under the right sun, sky, and wind just for the camera. Some of the photos taken that day were with a focal-plane shutter, others with a multispeed shutter.

Atlantic, 1933

Atlantic was not the only three-masted schooner sailing in the 1930s, but she was the leanest, the most agile, and with her ten sails against the clouds, the most beautiful.

Start Schooners, 1921

Large schooner-yacht racing reached its peak in the 1920s but ended in 1926. Often schooners, like the three shown here with *Ohonkaya* in the foreground, would start a race together. Symptomatic of the social changes that made the large yacht more difficult to maintain and race, a newspaper clipping of the time indicates that the crew of a schooner went on strike when asked to take the boat out for a Sunday trial run.

PART TWO

The Magnificent Js
1930~1937

*W*e feared that the stock market crash of 1929 would bring an end to the yachting world we knew and in which we worked. Many of the men whose yachts we photographed suffered grievously. Our studio on Nassau Street was just above the Wall Street district, and we were close enough to hear its sounds and feel the anguish. Surprisingly, really big yachts, the 200-footers, kept appearing. Contracts for them had been placed with builders before the crash, and many were completed. The sight of these new "floating citadels," as John Parkinson called them, helped encourage the idea that things were not that bad. I remember one morning when the bark *Hussar* (later *Sea Cloud*), the full-rigged ship *Seven Seas,* and the three-masted schooners *Migrant* and *Atlantic* were anchored just in front of our home on City Island, the sky filled with their yards and spars. Yachts were still being built and sailed, and our studio kept going.

In 1930, after a lapse of ten years and a long Prohibition era, America's Cup racing began again, even though it was the beginning of a depression. The first race was in 1930, followed by two more in 1934 and 1937. Gone were the gaff-riggers with their overhanging booms and long bowsprits. The new J-boats, tall, sleek, jib-headed sloops with mastheads rising as high as a fifteen-story building, dwarfed their crews on the deck below. *Ranger* (in 1937) was almost twice as long and had over five times the displacement of the 12-meter yachts racing today.

The Js were larger than life then, and in retro-spect they seem even more so. Just to see them hoist sail was an event. The sight of twenty men swaying on a halyard as the great mainsail quivered and climbed up the towering mast was almost unbelievable. There were bigger sailing ships to be seen, with masts almost as tall, but none with marconi rigs, which, on the J-boats, seemed like narrow slivers of white cloth piercing the sky and taking wing. In the world of yachting, the J class dominated the era.

The Js towered not only over the fleet, but in every yachtsman's imagination. Thirty years after the American Js were gone (broken up for scrap metal in World War II), when conversation turned to them, I would hear very vivid descriptions of how fast, how beautiful, how majestic they were. The class embodies much of the glamour, imagery, and romance of the America's Cup story. These boats were legendary both because of their size and power, and because of the people who sailed and designed them.

Harold Vanderbilt, skipper of the three defenders during the 1930s, *Enterprise, Rainbow,* and *Ranger,* was the scion of a wealthy Establishment family. He was a financier, a superb yachtsman, and the inventor of contract bridge, the card game that has fascinated millions. Charles Francis Adams, the taciturn New Englander, skippered *Yankee.* Descended of presidents, he was himself a former secretary of the navy. In a well-fought battle, he almost took the America's Cup defense away from Harold Vanderbilt in 1934. Starling Burgess, who designed the J-boats *Enterprise, Rainbow,* and, with Olin Stephens, *Ranger,* was the

1930s counterpart of Nathanael Herreshoff. Olin Stephens and his brother Rod were young lions just embarking on brilliant careers in yacht design.

In 1930, when he was eighty-two, Sir Thomas Lipton challenged for the fifth and last time with *Shamrock V*. In 1934 and 1937, the British challenges came from T. O. M. Sopwith, airplane builder, pilot, and developer of the famous Sopwith Camel in World War I. He skippered his two *Endeavour*s with skill and became a worthy adversary to Vanderbilt. The presence of these illustrious yachtsmen and their great yachts was felt on land and water from Boston to New York.

My father and I covered the racing off Newport in *Foto III,* which did 20 knots in calm waters, a speed that gave us a great sense of power as we moved around the fleet. On a day when the sea was rough, however, the J-boats would humble us. They drove on as though the waves didn't exist. Trying to keep up with the big Js in a seaway was so rough on *Foto* that we had to ease back on the throttle, and occasionally a *Rainbow* or a *Ranger* would show us her stern.

Yachtsmen kept active, and new yachts, both sail and power, appeared along the coast. In 1936 a one-design class was built by Sparkman and Stephens. The twenty New York Yacht Club 32-footers (45 feet overall) were built in 1936 in the Nevins yard on City Island. Also in about 1934, Bill Crosby designed and built a small Snipe, the first of a class now numbering many thousands.

As shown in these pages, the 1930s were a period of great diversity in sailing craft. In the course of a few days we might pass from a splendid schooner like *Migrant,* the biggest at that time, to an exquisite little ship like the square-rigger *Joseph Conrad,* which might be starting around the world on a voyage. The Chesapeake bugeye-yacht *Brown Smith Jones* would come into view with her raking masts shortly after passing *Rita Irene,* a well-kept little Nova Scotia schooner-yacht. In the ocean races to Bermuda and in the Southern Ocean Racing Conference, new designs stood out in marked contrast to the diverse character yachts that cruised nearby.

Compared with the tens of thousands of boats on the water between New York and Newport today, in the 1930s only a limited number of yachts were active. We knew almost all of these boats by name and photographed most of them. One of the reasons our file became so well-known is that we could pick from it almost anyone's yacht on demand.

Through the 1930s, most of our images were still on 5 × 7-inch glass plates or film, including all of the J-boat photographs here. The small format we used afloat was a 4 × 5-inch Speed Graphic. In 1938, when Kodachrome film became available, we began to use even smaller formats such as the Bantam, with which my father tried to become acquainted. The rest of us began to use the 35 mm camera, particularly with Kodachrome. We hardly realized it at the time, but the 35 mm camera and Kodachrome were shortly to effect a more radical change in photography than anything in the previous fifty years.

Yankee, 1930

Three syndicates from New York and one from Boston built America's Cup contenders. The Boston yacht *Yankee,* 125 feet, 6 inches overall, was average in size as well as performance in 1930, but raced well against *Rainbow* in 1934.

Whirlwind, Weetamoe, Enterprise

Under the new J-class rules in 1930, all contenders were tall, jib-headed sloops. The long, overhanging bowsprits and booms of the earlier gaff rigs were gone. *Whirlwind,* 130 feet overall, the biggest of the four new contenders, leads *Weetamoe,* 125 feet, and *Enterprise,* at 121 feet the smallest of the class.

Weetamoe

Weetamoe sends spray flying high over the deck as she smashes through a roller in Block Island Sound. Designed by Clinton H. Crane for the New York Yacht Club syndicate headed by Junius S. Morgan and George Nichols, *Weetamoe* battled with *Enterprise* through the trials but lost the honor of being selected as defender of the Cup.

Whirlwind

Designed by L. Francis Herreshoff, son of Nathanael Herreshoff, and built at the Lawley yard in South Boston, *Whirlwind* was a very different J-boat. She had the most displacement, was a double-ender with a tapered stern, and had a double-planked wooden hull. All the other J-boats built that year had steel frames with bronze plating. *Whirlwind* was for many yachtsmen a sentimental favorite, probably because she was built of wood, always an attraction to traditionalists. She not only looked different, she looked fast. Unfortunately, *Whirlwind* was never really in the running; she won one race in twenty-five starts.

Whirlwind

Whirlwind shows off her finely turned double-ended transom. The two photographs of *Whirlwind* were taken from *Foto* on the same day with a 5 × 7 Graphic from the same distance, height, and angle. They show how different a hull can appear when sailing on the wind and off. Opposite, *Whirlwind* sails almost level before the wind, with the lines of her long, white hull showing. The deck seems clear and simple. Above, close-hauled on the wind, *Whirlwind* is heeled rail-down, the lines of her hull are hidden, and her deck is a massive array of squares and curves.

Enterprise

Enterprise is rail-down and hard on the wind in a brisk sou'westerly breeze off Glen Cove, Long Island. Designed by W. Starling Burgess, *Enterprise* was the sixth successful America's Cup defender built by Herreshoff at the yard in Bristol, Rhode Island.

Conditions are exhilarating for the skipper and crew, but a stern view like this is wet going for the photographer. Flying spray gives both the photographer and his camera a bath as they poke outside the spray curtains and aim forward.

Enterprise Below Decks

Through the season *Enterprise* was often referred to as "the robot" or "mechanized yacht," a claim her skipper, Harold S. Vanderbilt, denied. He wrote that *Enterprise* was no more mechanical than any other contender. He believed that the reason people made this accusation was that he allowed photographs to be taken below decks and published. To Vanderbilt's experienced eye, the equipment seemed simple, though the photograph indicates otherwise, and *Enterprise* did have an eight-man below-deck crew. To the left are backstay winches and mainsheet spools with mainsheet brake. On the midship line, the boom downhaul winch is attached to the mast, and closer to the camera is the white wheel of the centerboard winch. Under the ladder are the handle and shaft for operating the on-deck jib topsail sheet winch.

Shamrock V

Sir Thomas Lipton, at the age of eighty-two, brought *Shamrock V* over for his fifth try at the America's Cup. His new J-boat was decisively beaten by *Enterprise*. Sir Thomas is reputed to have said at the end of his fifth try, "I canna' win, I canna' win." John Parkinson, Jr., in *The History of the New York Yacht Club*, published by the New York Yacht Club in 1975, quotes Ring Lardner: "There was hardly a dry eye in any American speakeasy."

Cresting Sea

The schooner *Flying Fish* scuds along in the trough behind a cresting wave as she runs eastward toward the Elizabeth Islands. In the 1930s and late 1940s, the stretch of open water between Point Judith and the mouth of Buzzards Bay of-fered us many of our most photogenic days. Usually we had a good sailing breeze, an active and interesting sea, and a variety of cruising and racing craft running to the east or beating to the west in the afternoon southwesterlies.

Mouette

The 12-meter class provided some of the best racing on the east coast and abroad in the late 1930s. At the time, more 12-meters were built in England, Scotland, and Scandinavia than in the United States. *Mouette*, an English-built 12-meter brought to Long Island Sound, is on an afternoon sail out of the Nevins yard at City Island. With sheets started, she glides on a crown of sparkling wake toward New Rochelle.

Sun on the water can gently twinkle, lightly sparkle, or violently glare. The range of dancing reflections is within most films' recording latitude, but when sparkle becomes glare, film is burned. We tried to expose for some shadow information, and we used a developer mixed for detail rather than contrast.

Chinook, a NYYC 40

In 1916 Herreshoff built twelve yachts of a new class, 59 feet overall with a 40-foot waterline. Raced hard for decades, they were called "Fighting Forties" when sailing prowess was discussed and "Roaring Forties" when the hard-driving crew and owners engaged in after-race partying. Husky and able, a few were later rerigged and went on to do well in ocean racing. Some of the class are still sailing today.

Black Dawn

My father was often up at dawn to photograph the rising sun over the Sound off City Island. He took this photograph from the sunporch in front of our house. His example started me off on a habitual sunrise reconnaissance that has lasted through my lifetime.

The wake of two vessels that passed up the Sound on a windless morning caused a pattern of ripples. Within a minute of the time this photograph was taken, a breeze sprang up and caused the sun to sparkle so strongly on the water that instead of little flashes of light, the reflection of the sun became a glare in the waves near the shore, destroying the delicacy shown here.

Dawn Under Mackerel Sky

The sun is rising behind a mackerel sky over City Island Roads. Both clouds and sunlight are reflected in the calm morning waters. The two powerboats moored in the right foreground are *Foto I* and *Foto III*. *Foto II* had been lost in a hurricane the year before.

Coastal Cruising

One of the thrills of cruising is the sense of freedom as the shore is left behind and open water beckons. A ketch leaves the thin line of its wake in the waters of Block Island Sound as it heads toward Montauk Point under a cloud-streaked sky. We spent most of our days afloat looking for the dramatic moment, but it was also a joy to encounter this kind of perfect serenity.

Weetamoe's Spinnaker

I spent most of the summer of 1934 in *Foto*, ranging the waters off Newport, never far away when the J-boats were racing. I had time to stay with the boats over long stretches of water and to pick moments when the sun, wind, clouds, or waves worked some particular magic on the boats. The power of *Weetamoe*'s parachute spinnaker is drawn by the sun in one sweeping curve.

Rainbow Launching, 1934

After *Vigilant* in 1893, the Herreshoff yard at Bristol had launched *Defender* in 1895, *Columbia* in 1899, *Reliance* in 1903, and *Resolute* in 1920. Now on a rainy spring day in 1934, *Rainbow*, 126 feet, 7 inches overall, the last America's Cup defender built by the Herreshoff yard, slowly slid down the ways.

Spectators

The J-boats stirred all sailors' imaginations. Often a large fleet followed them, at other times a very interested few. In the foreground, Junius S. Morgan, commodore of the New York Yacht Club in 1934 and a member of the America's Cup Committee, watches from his 70-foot commuter yacht, *Shuttle*. J. Pierpont Morgan, commodore of the New York Yacht Club in 1920 and a *Rainbow* syndicate member, was aboard his 343-foot *Corsair*, left. The object of their attention is the new J-class yacht *Rainbow*, skippered by Harold S. Vanderbilt.

Rainbow

Starling Burgess's new design for the Vanderbilt syndicate was as up-to-date and as
scientifically advanced as possible. However, the older *Yankee* with her refined
bow entrance proved to be a very fast
light-weather boat. At one point *Yankee*
outsailed *Rainbow* in ten consecutive
races. After changes in ballasting, *Rainbow* won the final elimination trials and
was selected to defend the Cup.

Yankee

Yankee, built in 1930, and her veteran
skipper, Charles Francis Adams, provided
a surprising turn to the 1934 trials when
they nearly won against the brand-new
Rainbow. Harold Vanderbilt, skipper of
Rainbow, wrote that *Yankee*'s speed
could be attributed to her new and
sharper bow and to the new sailpower
given her by a change in rig and a change
in rules. *Yankee*'s skipper, a taciturn and
reserved New Englander, kept the boat in
a racing trim that reflected his own taut
features.

Charles Francis Adams

Charles Francis Adams, skipper of *Yankee*, was slight of build but bold in body language, even at a distance. He almost always wore his white cotton hat. On this day we ran *Foto* close inboard and alongside in an attempt to obtain a characteristic photo of Adams at the wheel. Five minutes of such attention must have exasperated him, for without ever looking toward the camera, he called out, "Why don't you come aboard, Rosie?"

Under *Endeavour*

These views of an America's Cup yacht could be obtained only during a trial spin and only with the approval of the skipper. *Endeavour* was sailing for the photographer. My father was aboard and I was on *Foto*. I was permitted to get close under the windward bow and to throw *Foto*'s wake right under *Endeavour*'s lee bow, which would never be done under normal circumstances. One of these photographs served a special purpose: it shows only T. O. M. Sopwith and Mrs. Sopwith aboard, both at the wheel, a print we later gave them.

Endeavour

Vanderbilt thought that *Endeavour* was faster than *Rainbow,* an opinion widely shared. For a while *Endeavour,* sleek and powerful, seemed like a winner. Unfortunately for Sopwith, speed alone was not enough to lift the Cup.

Deck of Endeavour

Endeavour rolls into a little swell off Brenton Reef as a gentle breeze just fills her sails and moves her along at seven knots. T. O. M. Sopwith stands firm under the "Park Avenue" boom—so named because it was so broad that two men could walk on it. This type of boom was used on *Enterprise, Endeavour,* and *Endeavour II.*

Yankee, Rainbow Crossing Tacks

Yankee and *Rainbow* fought through the elimination trials of 1934, a cliffhanger until the end. *Rainbow* won the last trial race by one second. Earlier in the season during a dark northeaster, *Rainbow* crossed *Yankee*'s bow, a rare sight through most of the trials.

Rainbow Stern

A broad pattern of turbulent wake boils astern as *Rainbow* beats through a choppy sea in Buzzards Bay in the summer of 1936. Though our chase boat *Foto* was much faster than *Rainbow* in calm water, on this day *Foto* was hard pressed to keep up with the flying J-boat.

Rainbow

A *Rainbow* innovation was the "bendy" boom which could be curved by wires running alongside it to give an airfoil shape to the foot of the mainsail. Its height probably added a few square feet of unmeasured sail area. Although the J-boats were big and heavy, skippers paid great attention to the distribution of crew weight on board. The crew was on the rail when the wind piped up, as in the preceding photograph, and to midships and to leeward in light air, as shown.

The End of a Race

Endeavour's ventilated spinnaker frames the end of her hopes. *Rainbow,* at right, crossed the finish line and won the sixth race, the series, and the America's Cup.

Migrant Headsails

The headsail men aboard the three-masted schooner *Migrant* take to the foot-ropes under the long bowsprit to gather in the big jib topsail about to be lowered away. *Migrant* was built in 1929 and at 223 feet overall was hailed as the largest schooner-yacht in the world.

Riding a Swell

A large swell rolls toward the Rhode Island shore, helped along by a good southwesterly wind. With sheets started, a staysail schooner bound to the east rides the crest.

Chesapeake Bugeye

The bugeye, a local type of boat developed from working fishing schooners, was one of the bigger vessels in the oyster fisheries of Chesapeake Bay in the late 1800s. *Brown Smith Jones,* a yachting version of the bugeye, is a clipper-bowed, two-masted, leg-of-mutton-rigged, double-ended, centerboard ketch. Smaller, single-masted skipjacks still dredge for oysters on the bay.

M-Boats

The big M-class sloop *Prestige*, favored by a better-than-usual afternoon sou'westerly breeze, leads *Windward* in spirited racing off Glen Cove in Long Island Sound. The M class flourished in the early 1930s.

The photograph, taken from *Foto*, provides an excellent example of the advantages of a moving chase boat. *Foto* allowed us to find the best camera position for the composition of this photograph, one in which the distance between the boats is critical.

Dry Squall

The schooners *Water Gypsy* and *Nina* are knocked rail-down as a dry squall gusting off the Martha's Vineyard shore blows the wavetops off in a smother of white spray. The day was windy and the racing lively, but the heavy overcast was photographically discouraging. The two or three minutes of sunshine during which this photograph was taken lightened our spirits, as well as the surface of the water which, covered by flying spray, acted as a giant reflector.

Saraband

Saraband, built in 1906, was typical of the big schooners of that time. She was still racing here in 1936, beating westward along the Rhode Island shore en route from Buzzards Bay to Newport.

Queen Mab

The crew of the schooner *Queen Mab* take in her spinnaker the old way, manhandling it to the foredeck. *Queen Mab* is reaching along under balloon jib and balloon main topmast staysail, schooner-style.

Nina

For forty years the favorite east coast
ocean racer was the 59-foot staysail
schooner *Nina*. She was designed by Starling Burgess and built to sail in the transatlantic race to Spain in 1928. For decades
Nina seemed immortal; she was always
beautifully maintained and with her rig
redesigned again and again, she kept winning major ocean races. Rail-down with
spray flying, *Nina* is a symbol of the old
but able wooden ocean racer.

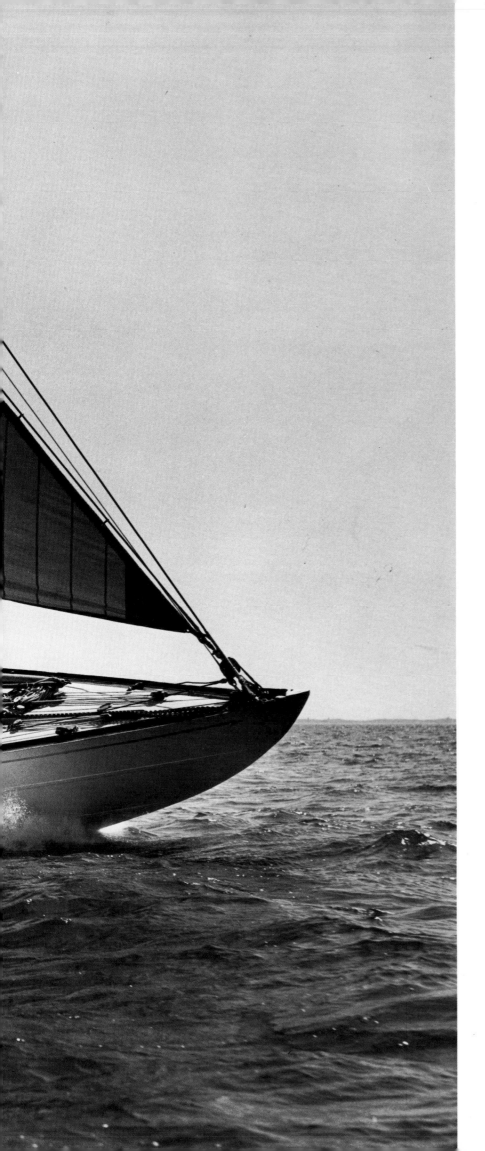

Weetamoe's Deck

There was no America's Cup race held in 1936, but three J-class yachts, *Rainbow*, *Yankee*, and *Weetamoe*, raced against each other off Newport, Rhode Island, seven times. *Rainbow* won two, *Yankee* won two, and *Weetamoe*, owned and sailed then by Chandler Hovey, had the best record with three wins. It was *Weetamoe*'s most successful season.

Rita Irene

The little schooner beating out of Huntington Harbor into the teeth of a blustery nor'wester is rising to a big sea and throwing it off in a halo of fine spray.

Joseph Conrad

On a frigid January morning in 1935, the *Joseph Conrad* sailed out of New York harbor with a crew of very young sailors aboard on a training cruise. The sails were frozen stiff, and the fingers of the crewmen aloft setting the topgallants were bloodied from clawing at sails and sheets. Against the afternoon sun the details are missing. What is left is the romance of the little square-rigger setting out to sea.

I took this photograph from the tugboat that assisted the *Joseph Conrad* away from the dock. The temperature was in the low teens. My fingers quickly froze, and the temptation to stay in the warm pilothouse became overwhelming.

Stormy Weather

Just after the start of the 1937 Miami-Nassau race, *Stormy Weather* is at the edge of the light-hued inshore water approaching the dark blue Gulf Stream. The 53-foot, 11-inch *Stormy Weather* was designed by Olin Stephens as a beamier development of his famous *Dorade*. Sailed by Rod Stephens in 1935, *Stormy Weather* won both the transatlantic race to Norway and the Fastnet Race.

Building *Ranger,* 1937

From 1893 to 1934, America's Cup defenders built at Herreshoff's yard were bronze-plated over steel frames. *Ranger*'s hull, 135 feet overall and built at the Bath Iron Works in Bath, Maine, was made of flush-riveted steel plates over steel frames. The cost was to have been borne one-half by Harold Vanderbilt and one-half by a syndicate to be formed by the New York Yacht Club. But the club could not put together a syndicate in 1937 as funds were in short supply, so Vanderbilt alone paid the bills. If the new *Ranger* had not been built, *Endeavour II* would surely have taken home the America's Cup.

Ranger

On an afternoon beat from Buzzards Bay to Newport, *Ranger*'s quadrilateral jib and staysail cast angular shadows on the luff of her mainsail. Her 165-foot mast soars majestically into the blue, held there by rod rigging that looks nowhere up to the task. She is one of the noblest creations of man, though the men on her deck look pitifully small by comparison.

There are times when clouds would add nothing to a photograph. Often the simplest statement is the strongest. The sharp, clean lines cast by the single light source are in stark outline where they highlight the sails. Even with less dramatic contrast, the shadowline of the mainsail's leach against the sky is bold.

Ranger's Bow

All during the summer, *Ranger*'s bow continued to be a source of conversation. A bow that buries itself in the water is usually an ungainly sight. Under full sail, *Ranger*'s bow settled in the water in a uniquely determined fashion. The sheer size of *Ranger* and the length of her bow can be measured by comparison with the figure of the mate crouched at the foot of the mast.

Ranger

Ranger is under sail in early June 1937, borrowing *Rainbow*'s mast and various rigging garnered from the sail lockers of *Enterprise*, *Weetamoe*, and *Vanitie*. This patchwork rigging held through the early trial racing until *Ranger*'s new mast was built and installed. In his book *On the Wind's Highway*, Vanderbilt wrote that *Ranger* was totally different from any other sailboat he had sailed. She was stiffer, gathered way more slowly, but held way longer, and when moving fast, just squatted down and went.

The early summer of 1937 brought weather to please a photographer. Days were fair, delightfully sketched with clouds at times, and a breeze kept the sails full and a white wake showing.

Ranger on the Wind

With sails trimmed and the quadrilateral jib drawing, *Ranger* heels to a freshening sou'westerly as she heads out toward Point Judith. One can tell from the clouds that the wind had been more in the northwest earlier in the day.

Backlighting emphasizes the seams in the sail and brings both highlight and shadow to the luff of the quadrilateral jib, giving the sail both fullness and form. The sun is high and falls on the foam at *Ranger*'s lee bow, throwing reflected light and a spot of contrast onto the hull.

Hoisting *Ranger*'s Main

All hands sway on *Ranger*'s main halyard
as a turn is taken around the winch aft.
The crewman in the bosun's chair is guiding the sail into the slides on the mast.
Ranger's crew was the last professional
crew to sail on an America's Cup defender.

Ranger's Afterguard

Harold Vanderbilt had a happy sailing season with *Ranger,* and some of his light-heartedness must have stemmed from the youth and enthusiasm in his afterguard, pictured here: Rod Stephens, Olin Stephens, Professor Zenas Bliss, Mrs. Harold Vanderbilt, Harold Vanderbilt, and Arthur Knapp. Vanderbilt, aware that their dress was not as formal as was customary aboard his yachts, referred to this as "the afterguard of *Ranger* in working clothes."

Ranger

Ranger started the season with *Rainbow*'s old mast, but she was fast even with the old rig. *Ranger* lost her own mast while being towed to Newport from Bath, Maine. After the mast failure, *Ranger* went through the season without serious problems. *Endeavour II,* built the year before, had already lost two masts in early sailing. The new J-boats were straining at their rigging and causing their fittings to fail.

At a certain point as the camera moves aft, the bow of a sailing yacht becomes foreshortened. The bow curves in toward the stem and the angle becomes more acute as the camera's eye moves astern. When photographing the hull from astern, we tried to settle at a point where the bow still looked powerful.

Endeavour I's Deck

T. O. M. Sopwith brought *Endeavour I*, which almost took the Cup in 1934, to Newport, Rhode Island, as a trial horse for his new *Endeavour II*. *Endeavour I* seldom raced, for the new *Endeavour II* proved to be much faster than her predecessor. In 1937 she was still beautiful under sail, but new design developments had passed her by.

Rainbow

Early in the 1937 season, *Rainbow* and *Ranger* raced spiritedly against each other. The beauty and power of the Js was fixed in mind during these early trials. *Rainbow,* passing Brenton Reef lightship, was obviously slower than the new *Ranger.* Symbolic of the J-boat past, *Rainbow* was still beautiful under sail.

Ranger

From her first trial spin, the 135-foot *Ranger* looked powerful and fast, more so than any other J. Her snub-nosed bow, not as fine as that of any of the other J-boats, and perhaps beautiful only to a loving eye, gave her the appearance of thrusting through the seas, invincible.

Start, Final Race

Ranger had no peer in speed and dominated the 1937 races. As a final fillip, Vanderbilt forced *Endeavour II* over the line a few seconds early at the start of the fourth race. The gun has just gone off and the starting line is marked by the buoy just over the stern of *Endeavour II*'s dark blue hull.

Endeavour II Restarts

A few seconds after the start, *Endeavour II* has turned around and is circling to get behind the starting line to begin again. *Ranger* led by four minutes at the first mark. As most yachtsmen had expected from *Ranger*'s performance during the summer, she won easily in four straight races.

On the Wind

In the most dramatic J-boat start in our files, *Endeavour I, Rainbow, Ranger, Endeavour II,* and *Yankee* are hard on the wind at a start in Buzzards Bay. These five historic yachts, all straining and alive as a yacht can be, will soon cross their last finish line.

Off the Wind

After the August Cup races of 1937, five J-boats raced against each other during the New York Yacht Club Annual Cruise. *Ranger,* with her 18,000-square-foot parachute spinnaker, leads *Rainbow, Endeavour I, Endeavour II,* and *Yankee* up Buzzards Bay before the afternoon sou'westerly.

Ranger and Lumber Schooner

The four-masted schooner with a deck-load of lumber, anchored off New London waiting for the tide to change and the wind to pipe up, offers a marked contrast to *Ranger.* Despite the seeming lack of wind, *Ranger* has enough way on under her parachute spinnaker to start white water moving along the side. The wind is just moving in with *Ranger* on the leading edge, as the ruffled water near her shows. We hardly realized when this photograph was taken that each vessel, in her own way, represented the end of an era.

The glassy water carried the strong contrasting reflection of the sails in a path right to the camera, intensified by the use of a deep orange filter.

J-Boats in the Fog

Rainbow, Ranger, and *Endeavour,* large as they were, come down to mortal scale in the fog off Buzzards Bay. The ghostly outline of another J is just discernible off *Endeavour*'s bow. Nothing in the rules or in the plans for future America's Cup races indicates that the big Js will ever sail back out of the fog or the past to race again for the America's Cup. However, today's maxi ocean racers are in spirit the Js of the eighties. At the moment this photograph was taken, *Foto* was almost as lost in the fog as the unidentifed ghostly J-boat.

PART THREE

Flying Spinnakers
1938–1964

*L*ife moved quickly between 1938 and 1941, both in the studio and on the water. The year 1938 was particularly significant, as "Flying Spinnakers," our most celebrated photograph, appeared full-page in *Life* magazine and brought a flood of mail from around the world.

The J-class was gone, but 12-meter yachts were very active and competitive. In good sailing and photographic weather, it was almost always rewarding to follow them, for hours if necessary. Somewhere along the way, at some buoy or at some shift of the wind, we were certain to find a photograph worth the chase.

We covered the round-the-buoy racing off Larchmont as regularly as possible, waiting out the time when wind and weather were right. There were so many starters and so many classes that it was only a matter of time before some quirk in weather or tactics would unfurl a few moments of dramatic action. The International One-Designs were a keenly sailed class, so we always tried to keep them in view.

In 1939 I saw one of the last great yachts of the prewar era sailing outside Block Island. In an image in this section, the 316-foot bark *Sea Cloud* rides on the path of the sun. Many of these ships were soon wearing navy gray.

The first of the post–World War II photographs here is the cruising/racing sloop *Valkyrie*, which serves as visual proof that for all the tragic disruption the war caused, it did nothing to diminish the joys a skipper could know at the tiller of his yacht in a spanking breeze. So we started again to capture images afloat that tell of pleasure, power, exhilaration, fatigue, dampness, isolation, camaraderie, and beauty.

After the war, the New York Yacht Club recognized that the America's Cup races would have to be sailed in boats smaller than the J class. As was necessary under the deed of gift, the club went to the courts to legally lower the waterline length of competing yachts to 44 feet. This change initiated challenges in 12-meter yachts. The British Royal Yacht Squadron declared their first 12-meter challenge in 1958 with the yacht *Sceptre*.

As anticipated when the blunt bow of *Sceptre* was first examined here by the American designer Olin Stephens, the defending yacht, *Columbia*, had an easy victory. While sometimes the outcome of America's Cup races is foreseeable, all of the challenges provide some moments of excitement, a twist or a triumph, a joy or a qualm, exuberance or memorable action.

For sheer drama, I think the most exciting moment in America's Cup history was when *Gretel* rode a giant swell, surfed past *Weatherly*, and then went on to win the second race in the series. That roaring ride was captured vividly through the telephoto lens on my 35 mm camera. This image would have been impossible twenty years earlier.

The 1958 and 1962 challenges were special for us. The New York Yacht Club Race Committee, in its infinite wisdom, gave us permission to maneuver with *Foto III* anywhere on the course during all the races without restriction, making *Foto* the only craft on the water with this privilege. The freedom this provided us in photographing the race can be appreciated only when compared to the restrictions imposed by the Race Committee today. Photographers, including myself, are now kept at great distances from the contestants and have had to resort to hiring helicopters in some cases. Those were not the good old days; they were the good close days.

The advent of the 35 mm camera and its battery of lenses brought a new intimacy to photographic reporting and a new version of America's Cup racing to the public. This little camera with its big lenses could capture the subtleties of body language, show the drained weariness of the winch-grinders during a tacking duel, and reveal the skipper's tension from his touch on the helm. It could even show the agility of the foredeck man from his fancy footwork on a spray-covered bow.

This camera could also reveal subtle differences in the way a boat heels or heads high, which indicates tenderness or pointing ability, often telling a story of victory or defeat. One photograph here shows *Courageous* pointing higher and footing faster than *Southern Cross,* which in this case foreshadowed the outcome of the race. In willing hands, the 35 mm camera becomes a vivid storyteller.

Crossing Spinnaker Tacks

Long Island Sound off Larchmont has been a busy thoroughfare on Saturday afternoons in summer since the turn of the century. In close quarters, an International One-Design bound for a turning mark and the 12-meter *Nyala,* headed for the finish line, cross spinnakers.

Five 12-meters started downwind in July 1938. *Northern Light* and *Gleam* in the foreground were soon paired off and aggressively engaged in their own match race. We followed close along with them. They were almost bow to stern as they raced along.

Spinnakers

We followed the three 12-meters *Gleam, Northern Light,* and *Nyala* for almost half an hour, first photographing them from windward and then moving to leeward where the curves of the sails enhanced each other. The third 12-meter, *Nyala,* was just astern, and we had to maneuver to keep from giving her our wake. To get the sense of sweep and the complementary curves in the sails to harmonize, we had to be precise in our timing, to be both in the right camera position and not in the wrong place for our wake. I was at the helm and would move into position, swing the bow, slow down, synchronizing our movements so that I could say, "Ready, Dad, ready—shoot."

Flying Spinnakers

The 12-meters *Gleam* and *Northern Light* are running down the Sound with spinnakers set under a clear sky and a growing southwesterly breeze. This photograph, taken in July of 1938, is probably the most-published Rosenfeld photo. It appeared full-page in *Life* magazine and inspired more mail than we had ever received before. In one day at our studio, we received letters from Bahrein, Capetown, and Rio de Janeiro requesting prints. It is a classic composition which speaks to yachtsmen and landlubbers alike. This photograph could only have been made in that decade, because spinnakers today are cut and set differently. Close-reaching, they would not form the soft, billowing curves seen on *Gleam* and *Northern Light.* The juxtaposition of sail on sail occurred for only a few seconds in this instance. When I saw it happening, the composition was so compelling that I moved in to catch the shot, regardless of our wake ahead of *Nyala.*

Zio and Nightwind

At the end of the 1930s we wondered if the J-boats would ever race again, as they had become too expensive to maintain. The smaller 12-meter class was becoming the yacht of the times. As opposed to the J-boats, the 12s had cruising accommodations below, so they could be raced overnight on cruises as well as day races. They provided most of the big-boat racing of the period. *Nightwind* and *Zio* are on a cruise from Glen Cove to New London and are reaching down the middle of the Sound well off the Connecticut shore in a freshening afternoon southwesterly.

12-Meters Around the Buoys

Three 12s are sailing a downwind leg close enough together to interact for the camera. The light on their sails is photographically ideal, with backlighting, highlighting, and curved shadows all at the same time.

Rainsquall Finish

A squall at the finish line off Larchmont lays down an unusual pattern of white rain on dark water. There is wind enough to drive the yachts along smartly and to whip the surface of the Sound into waves. The driving rain, however, smooths the wavetops, and the raindrops bouncing into the air are a smother of white that looks like mist on the meadows.

Deck *Nedumo*

Homeward bound, the deck of the yawl *Nedumo* is wet with spray, tossed by a fresh northwesterly breeze. *Nedumo* is heading up Long Island Sound toward Execution Light with the spires of Manhattan barely discernible to the right of the dark sail on the horizon. "*Nedumo*" was Henry Devereaux's abbreviation for "Never a Dull Moment."

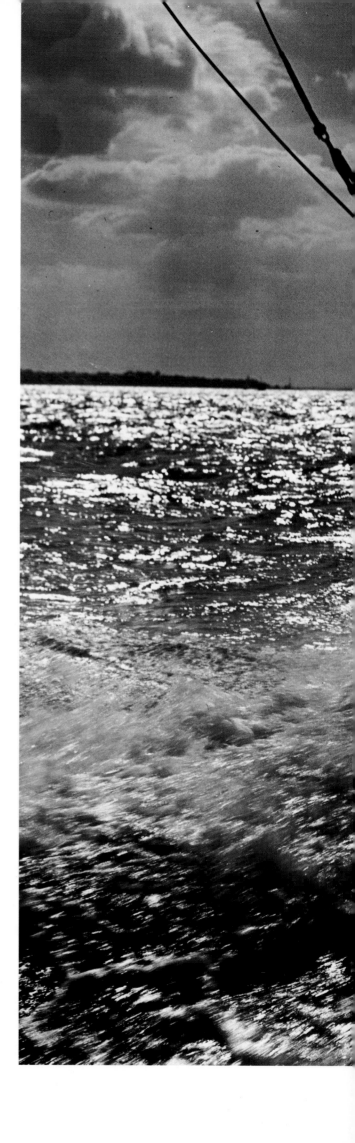

Sea Cloud

Under the noonday sun, the 316-foot bark *Sea Cloud* is sailing before a south-westerly breeze outside Block Island with twenty-eight of her sails set. These photographs were taken shortly before Ambassador Joseph E. Davies went to his posting in Russia in 1939. *Sea Cloud* accompanied him, carrying some of his personal gear aboard.

Mrs. Joseph E. Davies asked me to come to Newport to photograph *Sea Cloud* in September 1939. The captain had arranged for the charter of a venerable motor launch named *Champion* to

use as a photo boat. We waited for three days until a favorable breeze came up and then went out to sea with no communications between us, but a rendezvous place off Block Island selected. *Sea Cloud* disappeared over the horizon toward Montauk Point to set sails and get way on. As she approached and passed the chugging *Champion*, she seemed to be flying, probably making 17 knots to our top speed of 9. She was in camera range for less than five minutes until she sped away, not to be seen again until after World War II.

Cotton Blossom II Bow

The 12-meter *Cotton Blossom II* is beating to windward under a fresh breeze into a sea not heavy enough to slow her down, but big enough to send spray flying high over the weather rail. A sign of the strain on the rigging shows in the curve in the luff of the jib as the headstay sags off—no real problem, as the increased fullness in the jib helped to drive her through the waves. The old wooden 12-meters were strong and able yachts, and several became successful ocean racers.

Cotton Blossom II

The hull-wracking, rail-down action that created exciting photographs was not usual early in the spring in the era of wooden yachts. A cautious skipper waited until his wooden hull was well soaked and its seams were tight before putting this kind of strain to it.

We had a difficult time in the 1930s and 1940s trying to shoot a boat without the crew looking at the camera, which somehow always drew their attention. We often found it more rewarding to wait at a mark for the moment when the crew would be too busy to watch us.

Internationals Crossing Tacks

Three International One-Designs cross
tacks, port tack gives way, and as the
skipper pulls the tiller to windward, he
drives off to pass under the stern of the
starboard tack boats. Foam from the
wavetops is blowing in white streaks
along the direction of the wind, indicating
gusts in the high twenties.

International Knockdown

International One-Designs were sailed hard, and they sometimes carried spinnakers for longer than seemed logical. In a knockdown that had the crew climbing for the windward rail, both spinnaker and mainsail are dragging.

International Start

Skippers in the International One-Design class were sharp and very competitive, particularly at the starting line where every second counts. They usually hit the line with the starting gun.

International Spinnakers

Three International One-Designs are on a
close spinnaker reach on Long Island
Sound. The wind is in the northwest. Usually a few hours after a northerly weather
front moves into that area of the Sound,
cloud cover gets heavy. Here the clouds
are moving in, leaving an open spot of
sunshine overhead.

Valkyrie, 1946

The auxiliary cruising sloop *Valkyrie* is driving into a gusty southerly coming off the shore of Long Island. The rigging is taut, and there is tension in the out-stretched arm of the helmsman as he heads up slightly to ease the strain and free the deck of the water washing over the rail.

Mustang Reefing Main

Shortly after the start of the 1954 New-port-to-Bermuda race, the wind piped up and the crew aboard Rod Stephens's NYYC 32-footer turned a reef in the mainsail. Rod is well-known as a stickler for crew drill and for overall crew prep-aration.

Raven 31

A critical few moments aboard the Raven-class sloop *Vinky*. *Vinky* was on plane and creaming along as the spinnaker sheet parted. What now? Well, in the next installment the spinnaker took charge, went up into the air, and *Vinky* went over, dumping her crew.

Trouble

A spinnaker halyard slipped on the cutter *Julie*, the bitter end of the spinnaker halyard stopped at the masthead, and the spinnaker floated up and out. It snagged on a fitting atop the mizzenmast of the yawl *Merry Maiden*. *Merry Maiden* had trouble forward as well; her own spinnaker was set with a wrap in an hourglass bind. Both yachts sailed along in unwilling combination until a nimble crewman climbed *Merry Maiden*'s mizzen and cut the floating spinnaker free.

Fog at Buoy

When cruising along the coast, fog brings dampness, isolation, a feeling of anticipation, and even vague concern about the location of the next buoy. The clang of a bell and the sight of the buoy bring a sense of accomplishment that is heightened, of course, if the buoy is the one expected.

Fogbound

On a foggy morning, the Off-Soundings fleet stays at anchor. The yachts, rafted together to save space in a crowded anchorage as well as for companionship, provide a pleasant place to bide one's time until the fog lifts.

Rain

Torrential rain flattened the surface of
Long Island Sound, and dark, low clouds
threatened a squall. However, no rush of
violent wind swept the water as this fleet
of Luders 16s moved on without short-
ening sail.

Squall

Another year, another Luders 16, and another torrential rain, but this time a violent squall whips over the Sound. The crew dropped and secured the mainsail before the squall hit. The jib is torn and whipping about, but once the squall passed, the crew upped the mainsail and headed for the finish line.

OVERLEAF:

Ticonderoga

The racing fleet on the annual Miami-Nassau race crosses the Gulf Stream in winter, when sailing conditions can vary from a gale to a flat calm. The venerable 72-foot *Ticonderoga*, an L. Francis Herreshoff design built in 1936, is hull-down behind a big sea. This remnant of some distant storm has temporarily rolled the wind out of *Ticonderoga*'s spinnaker and mainsail.

Perfect Sailing Weather

Crossing the Gulf Stream can be a sailor's delight when the wind is southeasterly and the Stream kindly. At the start of a Miami-Nassau race, some of the yachts have a reef turned in, anticipating a rough passage. However, the wind ran with the Gulf Stream and the reefs were soon shaken out.

The Navigator

On a clear day with unlimited visibility, the water is smooth and all sails are filled and drawing. The navigator is forward, looking for a buoy, a mark of the course. He would like to see it pop up over the horizon dead ahead.

The camera was a 35 mm with a 20 mm wide-angle lens to catch the broad sweep stretching from the deck under the spinnaker to the horizon.

Good News

A brisk northwesterly was just the right breeze for a run down Long Island Sound. Both *Good News,* with a bone in her teeth and her spinnaker and staysail straining, and Prince Philip's dark yawl *Bloodhound* were moving at hull speed off Connecticut, bound for Newport, Rhode Island.

Heading East

The wind is north and the morning sun molds the form of the genoas of a cruising racing fleet as it starts a day's run heading east toward Buzzards Bay. The big, black, 73-foot yawl *Bolero,* owned by John Nicholas Brown, succeeded his schooner *Saraband.* Both were exquisitely maintained and a joy to every sailor's eye.

Christening *Columbia*, 1958

In 1958, after a lapse of twenty-one years, America's Cup competition began again. The great J-boats and their professional crews were gone. The new Cup competition was in smaller craft, 12-meter yachts about 66 feet overall and 45 feet on the waterline. Here Mary Sears christens the first new defender, *Columbia*, at the Nevins yard in City Island, New York. This event opened the new era with a magnificent champagne splash that left its mark on the sponsor as well as the times.

Columbia

Columbia, with sheets started, is roaring along. Briggs Cunningham is at the helm and Rod Stephens is riding high on the windward rail. Designed by Sparkman and Stephens and owned by a syndicate headed by Commodore Henry Sears, *Columbia* was closely matched in 1958 by *Vim*, sailed most of the season by Bus Mosbacher. *Vim* was an old boat built in 1939, and old boats are always favorites. Mosbacher and his crew sailed *Vim* so boldly and well that the keen competition between old and new caught and held the press and public's interest in the America's Cup.

Unloading *Sceptre*

Under the new rules, challengers no longer had to sail to the United States on their own bottoms. *Sceptre,* the British challenger in 1958, was shipped across the Atlantic on the deck of a steamer, unloaded in New York harbor, and towed up the East River to City Island.

Sceptre's Underbody

The new British challenger, *Sceptre*, proved to be a slow 12-meter. Olin Stephens, designer of the American defender *Columbia*, was standing next to me when I took this shot. He looked at the fullness of the bow section and said with a smile, "One of us must be wrong." As it turned out, Olin's *Columbia* was the better boat. In heavy seas, *Sceptre*'s round bow pounded into the waves. It was uncomfortable and slow going for the crew.

Weatherly in Frame

Three new 12-meter yachts were built of wood for the 1958 defense of the America's Cup: *Easterner* in Boston, *Columbia* at City Island, New York, and *Weatherly* at the Luders yard in Stamford, Connecticut. *Weatherly* is shown fully framed with the sheerstrake (the topmost plank) being installed. The frames, the ribs of the ship, were alternately of solid steam-bent oak and laminated mahogany. They were formed in the curves of the shape of the hull over pins that outlined their shape on a steel grid plate. The laminated frames were built up of quarter-inch strips of mahogany three inches wide in layers that were set in Bakelite glue to a depth of eight inches. After the laminated frames were set, they were sawed in half and became the port and starboard sister frames through the length of the hull. The horizontal strips shown are temporary stringers in place until the double-planked skin of the hull was applied.

A Swell

In summer months, the weather off Newport, Rhode Island, is usually moderate. Generally a place for good sailing with only little calm and some fog, Newport often has a brisk breeze and comfortable sea. On occasion, however, Block Island Sound is boisterous, or beset with swells from a distant storm rolling toward the shore. The foredeck crew of *Columbia*, sending up a genoa in stops, is almost hidden by the crest of a big, fast-moving swell. In 1962 this kind of swell surfed the Australian challenger *Gretel* past the defender *Weatherly* and on to a triumphant finish.

Sceptre Weather

The British challenger *Sceptre* lost the first two races of the four-out-of-seven series by large margins. The British explained their losses by saying that *Sceptre* was not a light-air boat; her day would come in heavier winds. At the start of the third race, the wind blew a strong 25 knots. The British boat won the start, but *Columbia* was two and a half minutes ahead at the first mark. Here *Columbia* is crossing *Sceptre*'s bow on the way to the windward mark. No weather seemed to be "*Sceptre* weather," after *Columbia* won four races straight to retain the Cup.

OVERLEAF:

Sceptre and Columbia

It could be said of *Sceptre*, flying her big French Herbulot spinnaker, in Shakespeare's words, "Beauty itself doth itself persuade." All *Sceptre*'s persuasion came to naught, for *Columbia*, with a sharper bow section and a smaller, very effective spinnaker, led *Sceptre* to the finish line in every race.

Gretel in a Northeaster, 1962

On a trial spin, the Australian challenger *Gretel* dips her pointed bow and slices into a sea during one of the three-day northeasterly storms that occasionally hit the New England coast. The wind was gusting well over 20 knots, just about the maximum for a 12-meter.

Gretel in a Squall

The crew is huddled well out on the windward rail as *Gretel* slogs through a nasty, short, choppy sea off Newport, Rhode Island. Jock Sturrock (at the wheel) and the drenched crew seem to relish plowing through the slop, reinforcing the hard-driving image of this first Australian challenge.

Drying Out

In 1962 all of the 12-meters were wooden yachts. Since wooden hulls soak up water, the 12s were often hauled out overnight with heaters set below to dry and lighten them. *Columbia*, *Nefertiti*, and *Weatherly* are drying out in Newport Shipyard with both the tide and the moon rising.

A Powerful 12

Gretel, designed by Alan Payne, was a powerful 12-meter, and each day she sailed off Newport brought some improvement in deck plan and performance. Here, with Jock Sturrock at the helm and the crew along the rail, *Gretel* shows her late-season racing form, clean and hard-driving.

Weatherly Lifting

Weatherly has thrust her bow through a big wave and now lifts high as water and spray cascade aft along the deck and under her genoa. The crew along the windward rail takes a bath. Bus Mosbacher is standing at the wheel in his usual aggressive stance.

Gretel

Gretel, though bigger in fact and sturdier in appearance than *Weatherly*, was more tender; her crew covered many miles draped over the windward rail as they are here, approaching the windward mark in a rough and building sea on the gusty day *Gretel* beat *Weatherly*.

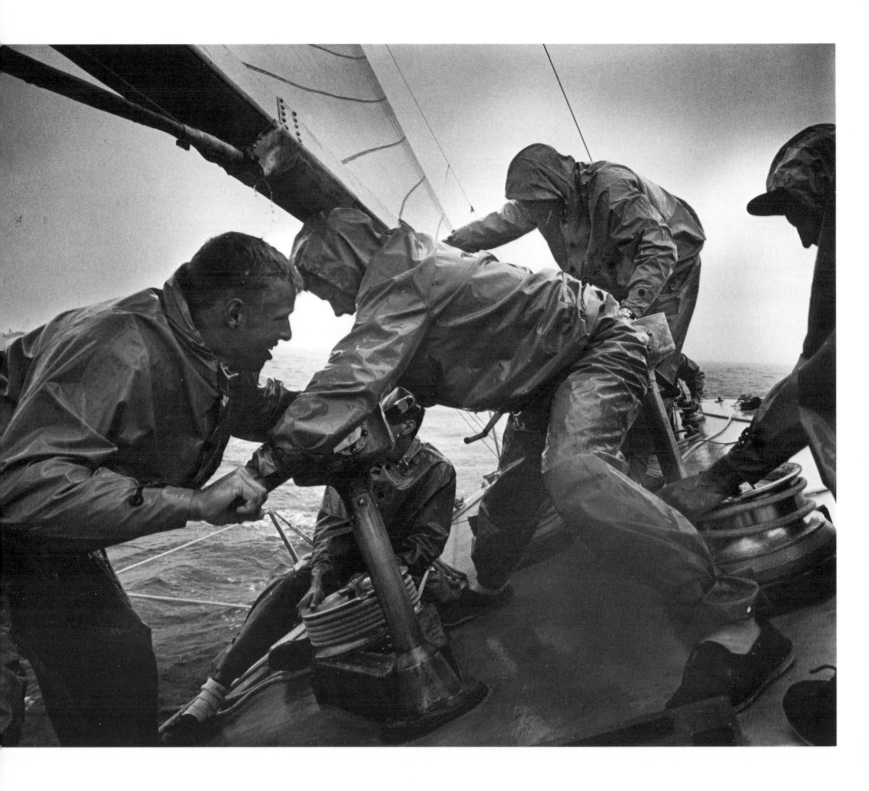

The Coffee Grinders

The grinders are the musclemen aboard 12-meters. A tacking duel can sorely try them as they are called upon again and again to match their strength and stamina against time, the power of the sail, and the pull of the genoa sheets. Here, aboard *Weatherly*, the rainy day does nothing to add joy to their job.

Sail Change

The wind is picking up and it is time for a sail change as the foredeck gang aboard *Gretel* takes in a jib. The man sitting on the pulpit unhanks the sail while the others smother it before passing it through the hatch and below. The low rail just a few inches over the deck does yeoman service as a heel- and toe-hold.

Gretel Surfing and *Gretel* Passing
Weatherly

Although I have photographed every
America's Cup race since the J-boats first
raced in 1930, the most vivid few moments of any race occurred on the last leg
of the second *Gretel-Weatherly* race in
1962. Just past the mark both yachts were
under spinnaker, *Gretel* trailing by fourteen seconds. Suddenly, a huge wave lifted
Gretel and she began surfing, moving very
fast. Then a second big wave lifted *Gretel*

high. With the crew's screams carrying
across the distance and a rooster tail
foaming from the shrouds, *Gretel* flew
past *Weatherly* into the lead and went on
to win. I suppose it is a common fantasy
for sailors to dream of their boats flying
through the air. *Gretel*'s surfing ride is the
nearest waking experience of this sort that
I have seen.

Gretel Chasing *Weatherly*

The year 1962 was a particularly rewarding one for the yachting photographer,
including wind, waves, sunshine, keen
racing, and the excitement the bigger-
than-life Australians brought to Newport
and America's Cup racing. Everything fit
together to the camera's delight. Just how
exciting Australia's challenge would be
was not fully realized until it came of age,
twenty-one years later, in 1983. Here
Gretel is chasing *Weatherly* and fighting
all the way. Except for *Gretel*'s moments
of glory in the second race, this spirit sym-
bolized the 1962 challenge.

Jock Sturrock

Sail seams are etched against the sky, sheets are straining, decks are awash, white wake is streaming astern, and salt spray tingles on the skipper's lips. Jock Sturrock, the helm alive in his hands, stands tall, outlined against *Weatherly*'s genoa. Though it may be bounty enough for a sailor to enjoy all the fruits of life and beauty, *Gretel* trails behind *Weatherly*, and for the skipper of *Gretel*, all's not right with the world.

The Closest Finish

In the fourth race in 1962, when the yachts were on a spinnaker reach nearing the finish line, *Weatherly* dropped her spinnaker and under her reaching jib worked up to windward. Just before the finish, *Weatherly* reset her spinnaker and with sheets eased, moved quickly past *Gretel* to win by twenty-six seconds, in the closest America's Cup race to date. Here *Gretel*, with spinnaker trimmed too flat, is passed to windward by *Weatherly*, a few hundred yards from the finish line.

Nefertiti's Spinnaker Staysail

With her big spinnaker set high and a big spinnaker staysail underneath to catch the air, *Nefertiti* is passing to windward of *Constellation*, whose afterguard is evaluating *Nefertiti*'s sails with more than aesthetic interest.

Constellation's Bendy Boom, 1964

With hulls glistening and water sparkling against early June sunlight, Ted Hood skippers *Nefertiti* around the windward mark ahead of Eric Ritter, who is seated at the wheel under *Constellation*'s new bending boom.

Northeaster

Constellation is racing from New London, Connecticut, to Block Island, with Bob Bavier at the helm. Though sheets are eased, the rail is down as *Constellation* heels under the force of a 30-knot easterly. Rod Stephens, standing with his right hand on the lower shroud, seems to be concerned about something up the mast. Usually smiling and cheerful, Rod has an instinctive ability to worry only at the right times. His concern was valid, as a few moments later the mast came crashing down.

Broken Mast

A few miles and a short while later, *Constellation*'s rigging failed and the mast snapped in two, a problem quickly repaired after a tow to Newport, Rhode Island. This day marked a turning point in *Constellation*'s fortunes, as she began to win consistently thereafter. What often happens among America's Cup contenders is expressed in the words of the sixteenth-century poet John Heywood: "A hard beginning maketh a good ending."

Port Jibe

Upwind and down, tacking and jibing, practice and drill again and again are wearying tasks through many of the daylight hours of the crews of America's Cup contenders. *Constellation*'s crew is squaring away on the port jibe, but very shortly the boom and spinnaker pole will swing across the decks again while sheets slap and winches clatter.

Sovereign

Cut in intricate patterns, the English challenger's brightly colored spinnakers were most pleasing to the eye. The sun glistens on *Sovereign*'s spinnaker as she reaches alone toward the next mark. Her rival, *Constellation*, is sailing alone too, but far ahead of *Sovereign*.

Start

At the starting line, *Constellation* sails across the wind toward *Sovereign*. The start was the only time the yachts were close together. *Constellation* footed faster, pointed higher, and took the seas more ably.

PART FOUR

On the Wind
1965–1983

*I*n recent years, yachting has flourished to such an extent that a yachting photographer must stay on the run just to keep up. As regattas, race weeks, championship series, and international events multiply, so do the craft in which people go sailing. Ideally, an overview of these two decades would include a child sailing alone in an Optimist Pram and a deck crew of twenty-four on a maxi racing yacht. Short of that, I have included a photograph of two children in a Penguin on the point of capsizing, and one of a maxi yacht racing in Hawaii with a crew of twenty-three on deck. The numbers may not equal the entire scope of crew lists, but I have tried to indicate the range of crew activity in the modern world of yachting and show some of the diverse vessels afloat.

Four of the photographs in this section were made with a $2\frac{1}{4} \times 3\frac{1}{4}$ camera put together from assembled spare parts. The others were done with 35 mm cameras, mostly with motor drives and an assortment of lenses with focal lengths ranging from 20 mm to 500 mm. If for no other reason, the 35 mm camera would have become a mainstay because of its portability and because it includes so extensive a variety of lenses, filters, and film, comparatively light in weight and bulk. It has proved a blessing, as along with my continued activity on the eastern seaboard, in recent years, assignments took me to Europe for months at a time and it seemed I was always carrying a camera outfit from one place to another.

Because of my training, I must admit I took to the motor drive on the 35 mm slowly. I remember the first assignment I covered on location for the studio was the docking of a steamship in 1928. I was given a 5×7 Speed Graphic camera and two plateholders, each with two glass plates, and I was told to bring back four publishable pictures. I had no room for error. The old, big-format cameras cultivated the discipline of anticipating and catching the significant instant on film with one quick shot. We had only one chance. By the time we changed our plateholder, any fast-occurring action was long over. The breaking of a bottle at a christening, crossing tacks, or spray flying all had to be thought of in terms of one exposure. It is possible to keep a motor drive going and sweep across the entire action. However, I still think of the motor drive principally as a fast rewinder that allows me to expose again immediately.

I have gone through many lenses and cameras through the years. Like people, cameras have a life span influenced by wear and tear. Salt water, as my cameras meet it, can be very destructive. A couple of years ago when cleaning out some filing cabinets, I came across nineteen 35 mm camera bodies, all of them frozen solid by the corrosive action of salt water that could not be attended to on location. Fortunately, camera replacements, when they are new models, generally have improved and interesting features.

Abandoning old ways has been painful at times. Although in 1978 I acquired *Foto IV,* my first fiberglass boat, I was reluctant to let go of *Foto III.* In 1979 *Foto III* was fifty years old, and maintenance took more time and thoughtful care than I could find to keep the wooden boat in proper form. My first thought was to bury her at sea with fitting ceremony. My wife Ruth, however, discouraged me as she felt that *Foto III* was one of the family and should be put out to pasture in an appropriate seaside setting. We gave her to a captain we knew with the hope that he would, as he said, care for the old girl faithfully. Though I miss *Foto III, Foto IV* has served me very well. She is a twin outdrive-powered 24-footer. Moored at Goat Island in Newport, Rhode Island, she has proved to be a very practical boat, with virtues that are essential to a photographer today: she is speedy, dry, and easily maneuverable.

After these many years cruising the waters on *Foto*, there are enough photographs in the Rosenfeld file to fill many books on a wide range of yachting subjects. I come back again and again to America's Cup racing because it holds a very special charm for me, as it did for my father. It is a contest with exquisite overtones. It is theater, drama, comedy, and tragedy afloat and ashore. It knows delicate nuances, broad farce, extreme dedication, and beauty. With each challenge, new stories unfold and old truths come back to haunt the course. I have photographed twelve summers of America's Cup racing, all of them since 1930, and I don't remember a dull moment. Foggy, calm, rough, wet—but never dull.

In 1967 Bus Mosbacher came back for his second defense of the Cup, this time in *Intrepid*, which won each race against the Australian challenger *Dame Pattie* by a wide margin. Robert W. Carrick and I did a book on *Intrepid*'s victory, and we interviewed each crew and syndicate member in great detail. Every one of their stories was absorbing, relating the complexity, talent, and dedication that go into a defense or a challenge. An entire book just begins to tell in depth one crew's story. It is the same for each challenge, win or lose.

In the photographs here I have touched a few notes to be remembered from each of the challenges between 1967 and 1983. A photograph of the Stevens Institute towing tank, where *Intrepid* was tested, symbolizes the growing influence of computer technology on 12-meter design, an influence that is sometimes dramatic, as in the case of *Intrepid* early in this section and *Australia II*.

Another image shows Bus Mosbacher, who was a fierce competitor, at the helm of *Intrepid*. When *Intrepid*'s mast snapped, it looked as limp as the broken wing of a bird. When *Intrepid*'s new mast was under tension, however, the titanium top seemed to fly again. In these pages, the foredeck crew of *Heritage* know at the same time the sun's glow on the water and the sorrow of defeat. *Courageous*, an aluminum skeleton inside, shows herself to be a curvaceous charmer outside. Photographs of the bowman, ducking under the spinnaker pole and calling the line, illustrate his lonely but critical role. Tacks are crossed, water sparkles, Ted Turner takes the spotlight, *Freedom* wins against *Australia*, and *Australia II* comes to Newport.

So much has been printed about the 1983 challenge that I thought it fitting to symbolize *Australia II*'s victory in time-honored fashion by showing her sailing into the sunset ahead of *Liberty*. Soon *Australia II*'s crew would carry the America's Cup home with them. They earned it.

Starboard Tack

Starboard tack has right of way, although it looks as though this starboard tack International One-Design is threading the needle's eye. They were close, as the tension in the bodies of the crews shows, but not quite so close as it seems to a 200 mm lens on a 35 mm camera.

It was a tense moment for the skipper sailing by the lee with his Penguin on beam end, and not the best of times to the crew scurrying toward the high lee rail. The worst of times was to come in a few seconds when the skipper did a flying jibe around the mark and almost capsized.

Hiking Out I

The crew hikes out to balance the force of the wind on the sail and so keep the hull on an optimum sailing plane. Crew weight hung outside the windward rail exerts the leverage. There is an art to hiking out, and to the searching camera it becomes a very individual exercise. Here, the alert tension of the skipper, Sandy Falconer, is a foil for the relaxed stance of the hiker, her husband, Bruce. Not even the seawater dripping from his bottom ruffles his poise.

Hiking Out II

The hiker sans hiking seat gets the most leverage from his outstretched body. If there is tension in his stance, see how delicately it is complemented by the skipper's gentle fingertip control of the tiller.

Hiking Out III

To some hikers, extended body leverage is not enough. The total experience involves a finger-clutching backward sweep of the head into the briny.

Hiking Out IV

Most hikers have a close affinity for the craft they crew on, expressed by the forward grasp or the derriere clutch.

Evening in Gulf Stream

It is the evening of a Miami-Nassau race, and we are almost halfway across the Gulf Stream on the way to Great Isaac Light. The sun is slightly more than one diameter over the horizon, and the burnished path of gold that streaks toward us across the water is almost gone. As the sun drops close to the sea, no path of light leads to it across the water.

After Dawn

The morning breeze is just stirring in this image. The sun, two diameters above the horizon, creates a path on the water under a warm glow and streaks the low clouds. The watch on deck is waiting for the new breeze to come alive.

Magic Carpet

Magic Carpet, a 56-foot yawl, barely has steerage way. A slight breeze stirs aloft, though no wind riffles the water's surface. Distant wakes have created the few waves that appear. They reflect the weak sun shrouded by high altostratus clouds. It is always a challenge to photograph the water's surface, to catch on film the nature of waves.

Mistral

A cold mistral in the Mediterranean off Marseilles, gusting to 40 knots, whips the wavetops off in flying spray. The surface of the sea all around us is broken by white combers. These reefed-down racing craft are accustomed to the blustery wind and sail through the day with no rigging failures.

Aries

Aries, just launched and bound for the Southern Ocean Racing Conference on a late fall day, is on her first trial spin down the Sound from the builder's yard at City Island, New York. Despite the biting cold, shipyard personnel, designers, sailmakers, and crew are along to see how it goes, and happy to be aboard. The first trial run is always a holiday.

Inverness

On a roaring reach off Nassau, Commodore Robert McCullough's big ketch *Inverness* lifts her bow and leaves her second wave astern as she flies toward the finish line off Paradise Island. The big canoe-type maxi-yachts are able to get up and go at surprising speeds.

Kialoa

The 80-foot maxi-yacht is an exquisite example of the fine arts that go into designing, building, and crewing the ultimate racing/cruising machine. They race on the east and west coasts, in the Mediterranean, in the Caribbean, off Australia—and off Hawaii, where *Kialoa* is reaching under spinnaker with a crew of twenty-three men on deck.

Spinnakers

Photographers expend a lot of time and effort afloat anticipating and rushing about to line up sails in graphic designs. But the photographer can achieve the same effect at his leisure in the darkroom, even on a cold winter's evening. All that is needed is the negative of a bow and a spinnaker, and time in the darkroom to reprint it in various sizes and sequential places.

Leaches

The leaches of these sails so rhythmically arranged in sunlight and shadow really happened out on the water, just as they are here. It took a lot of maneuvering, weaving, and dodging, as I moved from the helm to the rail with a camera, to arrive at the composition.

Crossing the Finish Line

A beam-to-beam spinnaker run across a finish line off Block Island means fast action for the crews, joy to the photographer, and confusion for the race committee.

Towing Tank, 1966

One of the models of a new design for *Intrepid* is making waves in the Stevens Institute towing tank. Tank-testing makes it possible to forecast the performance of a yacht and improve its design. The manner in which Cup yacht designers have interpreted testing results has made waves far outside the tank. *Intrepid,* with an improved hull, was a very successful 12-meter in 1967.

Bus Mosbacher

Emil "Bus" Mosbacher, Jr., successful skipper of *Weatherly* in 1962 and *Intrepid* in 1967, was a fierce, competitive, and untiring helmsman. He sailed every race as though his life depended on it. He always looked intensely involved with the moment, but in his mind he was planning the next three moves.

Intrepid's Deck

Intrepid's deck was very clean. With the coffee grinders down below, the winch tailers could work from hatches in the deck. This was a good way to get weight down low. It moved most of the crew out of camera range, however, which was no improvement at all from the photographer's point of view.

Knockdown

A knockdown in a squall sent water rushing along *Intrepid*'s deck as though the foot of the genoa were scooping it aboard. It is difficult to show this much action and excitement aboard a 12-meter, and for this reason I like the photograph. However, Bus Mosbacher, who was at the wheel, thought I should never show this print. Bus said, "It is no way to sail a 12. Squall or not, there is too much water on the deck."

Broken Mast

Sails are not always filled and curving against the sky, and masts do not always reach toward the heavens. Slimmed down to save weight aloft, *Intrepid* twice lost her mast in 1967. Here, the mast has snapped at the lowest spreader and a section of the bar rigging arches along the deck. When I heard the mast snap, I thought of the bar rigging slashing about like a knife blade, and I very quickly dove into the aft hatch.

Deck of *Dame Pattie*

Dame Pattie, the Australian challenger in 1967, had her coffee-grinder winches on deck, and the burly crew was up there to be seen. Boats are beautiful, and to me, purposeful people enhance their beauty. Even though they are losing this race to *Intrepid*, *Dame Pattie* and her crew look right to the camera.

Dry Nor'easter

The day before hurricane Doria moved along the New England coast, a 16-knot dry nor'easter gave *Dame Pattie* a chance to live up to her vaunted heavy-weather ability, but the Australian challenger found the going tough and was no match for *Intrepid*. In the distance, Mosbacher kept *Intrepid* moving out and to windward.

Windward Work

Afternoon sunlight dapples the water at the outer mark. *Intrepid*'s bow sends spray flying, her spinnaker pole casts a strong shadow across her genoa, and masts converge sharply as *Dame Pattie* heels more to the wind.

Titanium Tension, 1970

In 1970 the dark top section of *Intrepid*'s mast and the bar rigging were made of titanium, and the lower section of the mast was aluminum. It is difficult to show the strain on rigging, but in this photograph the arched mast captures some of the tension.

Soft Glow

Backlighting on the water and sails and a dark shadow of bodies against the sea lend charm and a touch of romance afloat, so that sometimes the real message of the moment is all but lost in the glow. Here are two such photographs, similar in lighting but telling different stories. On the facing page, *Intrepid* is triumphant. Above, the foredeck gang on *Heritage,* which has lost almost every race during the season, watches its rival sail on ahead into the setting sun.

Aluminum Frames, 1974

The America's Cup races originally scheduled for 1973 were postponed until 1974 to allow both defenders and challengers time to take advantage of the rule change that allowed 12-meter hulls to be built of aluminum. Previous 12-meters had been built of wood—mahogany planking over laminated oak or maple frames. Facing forward below, it looks as though the new defender *Courageous* is more missile than yacht.

Intrepid, Courageous

The old wooden 12-meter *Intrepid*, lightened at the ends and restored toward her original lines, fought *Courageous* through the trials, right up until *Courageous* was selected on September 2 to defend the Cup. Here, *Intrepid* is to windward of *Courageous* and holding on. Their rivalry was the big America's Cup story in 1974.

Courageous

On the wind, *Courageous* was almost a ghost ship. Coffee-grinder winches were below, so most of her crew worked beneath the decks. For long stretches, just an occasional head popped out of one of the hatches.

Courageous's Hull

With a crease at the waterline astern, a small rudder, a big trim tab aft on the keel, and long, low, balanced overhangs, *Courageous* had a bottom that drew admiring audiences.

Bowman

The bowman has the loneliest job on a
12. He must have precision timing on a
spinnaker jibe, and muscle when a genoa
is set. He has to be able to duck his head
and at the same time keep his footing, no
matter how wet or slippery the deck.

Calling the Line

The bowman on *Courageous* is calling the
line and keeping track of *Intrepid* as they
maneuver in close quarters at the start.

Southern Cross and *Courageous* in Mist

Block Island Sound is not all sunshine and fair wind. Fog and heavy mist are to be expected. Here, *Southern Cross* trails *Courageous* on a day when mist is heavy over the water, but visibility is fair and the horizon is clear. In one image we have the story of the race: victorious *Courageous* up ahead is pointing higher and footing faster than the challenger, *Southern Cross.*

Fog

Later in the same race, the mist has given way to fog. The horizon is gone, and *Courageous*, leading *Southern Cross*, is on the edge of visibility. Shadows on the sail show the sun shining through the fog.

Sunset

On one of the few days the sun set on an America's Cup trial, *Courageous* and *Intrepid* approach the finish line as the sun touches the top of *Courageous*'s mast.

Enterprise Crossing *Courageous*, 1977

Enterprise, a new 12-meter in 1977, crosses the bow of veteran *Courageous*. Though both are in shadow, *Courageous* and skipper Ted Turner soon took and held the limelight. Turner, like Sir Thomas Lipton at the turn of the century, had a remarkable ability to attract favorable press coverage.

Crossing Tacks I

Near the windward mark, *Courageous* on a port tack crosses *Independence* against a swirl of sunlit waves. If there is a racing breeze when facing against the sun, the waters of Block Island Sound come alive as every ripple glistens.

Sverige

The Swedish 12-meter *Sverige* under spinnaker sails with the sun. Deck and sails stand out clearly, but just the foam of the wake and little whitecaps show on the dark surface of Block Island Sound. Facing with the sun, wind and wave signs on the water are missing.

Courageous and *Australia*

In 1977 the American defender won four straight races from the Australian challenger. Most of the excitement and news that year were in the trials, not the final races. Here *Courageous* is to windward and ahead of *Australia* on a dull, overcast day.

Ted Turner

It seems that a spotlight shines on Ted Turner at the helm of *Courageous*. Nineteen seventy-seven was his summer at Newport, where he was always center stage. The boldest image that remains in my mind is of Ted Turner at the helm with another 12 crossing his bow, but you can just bet Turner will be ahead at the finish.

Crossing Tacks II

The America's Cup races are match races between two 12-meter yachts. Some days they are too far apart for a photographer to obtain an image of spirited contest. However, his adrenalin is pumping when the yachts are about to cross tacks. I am to leeward of both *Courageous* and *Independence*, and though they are obviously sailing clear of each other, there is enough action in the clashing diagonals of their rigging and hulls to make me happy.

Turner at the Helm

Ted Turner was unpredictable, newsworthy, and successful as a defending skipper in 1977. He was a great raconteur, helmsman, and the cynosure of all eyes at Newport, both afloat and ashore. Here he shows the intensity for which he is famous.

Freedom, 1980

Freedom, reaching under spinnaker, dips her boom end under to raise a rooster tail. Dennis Conner is at the wheel, standing tall as he did all through 1980.

Freedom and *Australia*

The year 1980 was the America's Cup of the bendy mast. *Lionheart,* the British challenger, brought over the innovative rig—the top third of her mast was fiberglass and could take an extreme bend. The bend gave the mainsail extra sail area and more power in light air. *Australia,* the challenger, adopted the rig just before the Cup races started. Here, in the second race, *Australia,* showing her bendy mast, crosses ahead of the defender *Freedom.* To the right, *Australia* takes advantage of a lift as *Freedom* tries to drive through her lee. *Australia* won this race by twenty-eight seconds, but *Freedom* won four out of five to retain the Cup. *Australia* was a stronger threat in 1980 than the results would indicate.

Defender—US 33, and *Liberty*—US 40 maneuvering before the start of a trial race, leave the circle of their wakes in the sunlit water of Block Island Sound.

Challenge 12 and *Victory 83*

Victory 83, the British challenger, leads the Australian *Challenge 12* at the mark. The bowman is out at the end of *Victory 83*'s spinnaker pole in an unusual and acrobatic maneuver to release the spinnaker.

Freedom and *Liberty*

Freedom, the 1980 defender, and *Liberty*, 1983 defender, sail in a close spinnaker reach near a leeward mark on one of their almost-daily sail drills.

Genoas

Sunshine through the genoas of *Australia II* and *Liberty* highlights their variety of vertical and horizontal panels in the new Mylar and Kevlar fabrics.

Mylar and Kevlar

In 1983 sails were of Mylar, Kevlar, and Dacron in different combinations and strengths, with panels cut vertically, horizontally, and radially. They made new designs afloat for the camera. *Australia II*, to windward of *Liberty,* remained there until the finish.

America's Cup Winners

John Bertrand, skipper of *Australia II,* and Alan Bond, owner, admire and embrace the America's Cup at the awards ceremony at Marble House in Newport, Rhode Island.

Winged Keel

Whether or not there is magic in *Australia II*'s keel, the winged slug of lead helped lift the silver ewer that had rested for so long in the New York Yacht Club. It was a wonder to behold when finally unveiled.

OVERLEAF:

Australia II Leads

On the wind, *Australia II* leads *Liberty* across the golden waters along the sun's sparkling path to finish first. As another first to add to her laurels, *Australia II* took home the America's Cup.

PART FIVE

Strong Winds Down Under

1984-1987

The sport of yachting continued to flourish in the 1980s. Big maxi ocean-racing yachts increased in number and sophistication; long ocean voyages proliferated, both racing and cruising; transatlantic and round-the-world singlehandled races—a sport that attracts a very particular kind of sailor—crossed and recrossed the oceans. Large multihulled craft built of exotic materials and equipped with rigid sails modeled after airplane wings cut through the ocean waves and roiled the waters of the America's Cup scene. Sophisticated motoryachts increased in number and the new class of 30-knot water-jet-powered 100-footers flashed on the waters between the Arabian Gulf and Fort Lauderdale, Florida.

The yachting event that most captured the interest and imagination of people everywhere occurred off Western Australia. America's Cup racing excitement built up over a period of four months from October 1986, until the finale on February 4, 1987. Thanks to the instant communication of television and the technical advances in photography, armchair sailors were able to feel the same excitement and surge of adrenaline experienced off Fremantle by the crews sailing aboard the 12-meter yachts in pursuit of the America's Cup. The twenty-four new photographs featured in Part Five were made during those four months.

Fremantle brought a new kind of sailing to America's Cup racing. There was more wind, more wave, more color, and generally more excitement to the water. In addition, the 12-meters were newly designed to cope with the strenuous conditions, so they sailed boldly through waves that would have daunted all of the previous generations of 12s. There was daily drama both afloat and ashore.

For the first time in America's Cup history, teams from the United States were trying to win the Cup back. More to the point, Dennis Conner, who had lost the Cup in 1983, was making his own particular waves in Australia. His consuming desire to win was a rich lode for the press. His passionate search evoked actions that alternately won him the grudging admiration of most Australians and the enmity of most New Zealanders. Almost everything he said and did was news, not only Down Under, but in the rest of the yachting world, which now seemed to be everywhere the airwaves or press could reach.

The thousands of journalists who came to Fremantle provided coverage worthy of the Olympics. Yachts were competing from England, France, Italy, Australia, New Zealand, Canada, and the United States and before the racing was over, Japanese, Swedish, German, Swiss, and Spanish yachtsmen, among others, were on the scene, purportedly preparing for future challenges from their own countries.

To all assembled at Fremantle, sailors, press, and spectators alike, the races were great theater as well as great sport. Gage Roads, where the racing was held, was itself a stage where nature provided all the necessary props. Normally a swell coming in from the Indian Ocean crossed the course at right angles to the wind-driven waves. The combinations of waves and strong winds made for spectacular sailing. Some days the distance between wave crests would provide deep troughs for the 12s to slide into. Other days, the distance between crests was just about the length of a 12-meter, so when the stern was lifted by one crest, the bow would be diving into the next. Occasionally, big waves washed across a deck and swept men and equipment into the Indian Ocean.

There are no safety rails on 12-meters, so the foredeck crew had to work in conditions that required extreme skill just to stay aboard. It made for exciting photographic coverage, for still photographers as well as television crews. In addition to the action in flying spray and heaving decks, the body language of the crew spoke of tension and danger. For icing on the cake, the natural light above was vibrant and crystalline, and the water below changed from pale green to vivid turquoise. Standing out boldly against the brilliant blue sky were sails cut in technologically new patterns and spinnakers in colorful bands. There had never been so much to stir the senses afloat, though many otherwise ardent spectators begged for a reprieve from seasickness.

The major story at first was the attempt by the United States to regain the America's Cup, but there were very soon a multitude of subplots. Each of the thirteen challengers had its own story. *Courageous*, plagued by a lack of funds and speed, dropped out at the beginning. Among the twelve to survive into the racing were two Italian boats, each representing a different aspect of Italian style and culture.

Azzurra again represented the Aga Khan and the Costa Smeralda Yacht Club, which was the Challenger of Record. It very ably ran the challenge series, a gigantic task when we consider that through the three Round Robins, the semifinals, and the challenger finals, 223 match races were run between the challengers. It is to the race committee's credit that all were run competently and smoothly, a superb organizational effort very much appreciated by all the participants and the press. The challenger series was called the Louis Vuitton Cup and was generously supported by that company.

Italia, the second Italian challenger, represented the more traditional Genoa Yacht Club, but managed to include a noticeably stylish presence with sailing outfits courtesy of Gucci, one of its sponsors. The Italian effort again brought flair to the challenge. Though appreciated by all, this unfortunately did little to help their sailing record.

The British challenger *White Crusader* always seemed on the edge of a performance breakthrough, a belief encouraged in brilliantly verbal fashion by its skipper, Harold Cudmore. Results were not realized in time to get the British into the semifinals.

The Canadians, after a difficult beginning beset by financial problems, brought *Canada II* to Fremantle. Although a craft with many friends, it too was late in developing.

French Kiss, on the other hand, although the name might appear facetious, was a good boat sailed very seriously. It had comparatively few breakdowns, improved as the season went on, and was one of the four competing challengers to reach the semifinals.

New Zealand moved into the big time very quickly. It was the only fiberglass hull, it had the youngest skipper, and the head of its syndicate, Michael Fay, was a hard-driving, determined, and brilliant strategist. He left his mark on America's Cup racing that will be felt for years to come.

Of five American challengers, three did not reach the semifinals. *Heart of America*, a mid-continent effort, stretched the rules a bit in order to have Lake Michigan declared an arm of the sea in the sense intended by the Deed of Gift. It was a much-loved craft with a highly respected and well-liked skipper, Buddy Melges. Though *Heart of America* did not achieve its desired goal, it was cheered all along the way.

Eagle, from Newport Beach, was one of the three California challengers. It carried the most striking logo in the fleet, a huge eagle painted broadly on each side. The expression of the eagle was the fiercest aspect of that challenge and certainly added a distinctive presence to the racing.

The New York Yacht Club's challenger, *America II*, skippered by John Kolius, was shipped out to Australia well before the racing, so the crew could drill in the conditions that prevailed on the actual course. Despite the most meticulous preparation and arduous practice, *America II* was defeated by *New Zealand* in one of the most dramatic confrontations and lost a place in the semifinals to *French Kiss* by the merest of margins, 128 points to 129.

USA, from the St. Francis Yacht Club in San Francisco, skippered by the irrepressible Tom Blackaller, was an innovative design that on occasion seemed to have great speed potential, but like a high-strung horse, required a deal deal of fine tuning. Although the tuning never seemed completed, *USA* did race in the semifinals, to be beaten there by *Stars and Stripes*.

Stars and Stripes, representing the San Diego Yacht Club, with star skipper Dennis Conner at the helm, was the culmination of a long research and development program and rugged preparatory training off Hawaii. The design was based on the belief that the boat with the fastest straight-line speed would triumph off Fremantle. They achieved the desired speed and that, combined with the expertise of their champion skipper, proved to be the winning combination.

The Australians conducted their own elimination series to select one from among six defenders. They sailed 93 trial races and on the shore conducted a series of personal confrontations, principally between the veteran challenger Alan Bond and Kevin Parry of rival syndicates. The fireworks ashore were more spectacular than the defense trials afloat and gave members of the press much more to write about. In the end, *Kookaburra III* of the Parry syndicate outsailed Alan Bond's *Australia IV* to be selected as the defender.

The America's Cup races between *Stars and Stripes* and *Kookaburra III* resulted in a clean four-zero sweep for the Americans. It was filled with the special drama America's Cup racing has always aroused, but the hottest competition of the racing off Fremantle was the earlier elimination contest between *Stars and Stripes* and *New Zealand*. *New Zealand* may even have had an edge in speed, but Conner conducted a perfect campaign and had the edge in experience when that quality was necessary to win. Off Fremantle, the America's Cup captured interest around the world with its most dramatic spectacle to date. The pot is boiling and once again we see speculation, confrontation, and litigation about the future of the America's Cup.

America's Cup Buoy off Fremantle

Bobbing in Gage Roads during the Louis Vuitton Fleet Race is the Royal Perth Yacht Club's own America's Cup buoy, modeled after the one that served at the start of America's Cup 12-meter racing off Newport, Rhode Island. As a proprietary touch, the yacht club had added cutout silhouettes of the Cup itself.

Wind on the Water

Swells coming in from the Indian Ocean crossed the wind-driven waves in a pattern of dancing reflections and dark streaks of wind on the water. Even on the downwind legs, traditionally the least interesting, the 12s looked lively. Here, *Canada II* heading for the leeward mark casts the shadow of her sails on the water.

First Fiberglass 12

From the very first race, *New Zealand* became the boat to beat. The only fiberglass 12-meter in the fleet proved to be fast, maneuverable, and well handled. From the air it looks long and lean as it slices easily through the waves. Crew work in the early races was highly efficient, and the combination of boat and crew built up an image of invincibility that lasted until their final defeat by Dennis Conner in *Stars and Stripes*.

Crossing Tacks III

Just after the start of the third race of the America's Cup finals, *Kookaburra III* crossed ahead of *Stars and Stripes*. For the photographers, it was a great moment with a chance to capture a crossing tack situation. *Kookaburra III* managed to repeat this crossing three times in the early minutes of the windward leg before *Stars and Stripes* drove through her lee and took the lead.

Diving into the Trough

Approaching the weather mark, the hull of *Canada II* disappears as it dives into a trough. The crewmen appearing above the crest of the nearer wave seem to be floating in flying spray. Astern, *USA* crosses *Canada II*. The wind at this time was blowing over 30 knots and the 12s were sailing in conditions that would have meant a cancellation of racing in previous years.

Two photographs of *Eagle* made within a few seconds of each other show how dramatically different the 12s could appear to the camera. On the left, *Eagle* in the trough of the seas is smashing through a wave with spray flying over the deck. Only a few feet of the hull appear, and the crew is hidden by the wall of water. The 12-meter looks very puny. Below, a few seconds later, after scattering the spray and lifting out of the crest of the wave, *Eagle*'s hull is revealed with the striking logo of its fierce namesake. In this photograph, the 12-meter surges powerfully through the seas.

Settling into the Trough

After rounding the jibe mark late in the afternoon of a day when the Fremantle Doctor was blowing hard, *Stars and Stripes* settles in the trough. The mark rounding has gone smoothly and though the hull looks as though it might be diving under the waves, all is well aboard as *Stars and Stripes* heads for the leeward mark.

Spinnaker Trouble

Heart of America has rounded the same jibe mark and though the same sun shines down on them, the crew is struggling to overcome a series of disastrous blows: a man has gone overboard, two spinnakers have been destroyed, and the spinnaker pole has cracked near the end. In the boisterous conditions at the marks off Fremantle, the photographers as well as the crew had to be alert as the fortunes of the yachts racing changed from one moment to the next.

Jibe Set in Shadow and Jibe Set in Sun

On the left, *Stars and Stripes* is setting spinnaker as she jibes after rounding the windward mark to head back down the course. Here the photo boat is to leeward of the mark; the sun, coming through the sails, provides strong, contrasting patterns in the sailcloth and in the dark silhouettes of the foredeck crew. Alan Bond's blimp with cameras aboard appears between the spinnaker and the genoa. To the right, at the same mark on a different day, *New Zealand* goes through the same maneuver. This time the photo boat is on the sunny side of the weather mark and when the jibe is finished, both the crew and the sails will be in more uniform sunlight. It was always a considered decision for the photographers to determine from which side of the mark the more interesting photographs could be made.

Rounding the Jibe Mark

Canada II is rounding the jibe mark and her spinnaker pole is starting to swing across the foredeck. It is a critical few seconds for the bowman, who has wrapped himself around the headstay for support. In the usually strong winds off Fremantle, rounding this mark was always a tricky maneuver, often carried out under great pressure. The skilled crews usually executed it very smoothly.

Reaching

Near the end of a reaching leg, in the moments of her greatest glory, *French Kiss* leads *New Zealand*. From the third to the seventh mark, *French Kiss* stayed ahead, only to be beaten by *New Zealand* on the gruelling last windward leg. Here, close to the mark, both yachts are setting their genoas under their spinnakers. *French Kiss* sailed through the series with few mishaps and competent crew work; she was an underdog favorite right into the semifinals.

Spinnaker Release

Heart of America is leading *French Kiss* as they approach the leeward mark on the second leg. Both have their foredeck men up in the air at the end of their spinnaker poles in a maneuver that released the spinnakers and gave the photographers a chance to show acrobatics aloft. Aboard *Heart of America*, the spinnaker has already been released. The next time they rounded this mark, *French Kiss* was ahead and sailed on to win the race.

Coming About

America II follows *New Zealand* around the mark to the last windward leg of the critical race that saw *America II* eliminated from competition. Just fifty-two minutes earlier, *America II* had led *New Zealand* around this same mark, holding grimly on to her final chance to sail in the semifinals. *New Zealand*, however, worked inexorably ahead on that leg and led to the finish. Here they are thirteen seconds apart, the difference that meant for the first time in its history, the New York Yacht Club's craft would not race in the America's Cup.

Downwind

Stars and Stripes leads New Zealand around the leeward mark in the first race of the challenger finals. To many observers in Fremantle, New Zealand seemed the faster of the two, but in the first race of their crucial series, Stars and Stripes started ahead and stayed there through every leg of the course.

Close-Hauled

In the third race of the challenger finals, Stars and Stripes led around the first mark, but soon after lost her spinnaker and New Zealand forged ahead. Here, on the second windward leg, New Zealand to windward is stretching out the six-second lead she held at the leeward mark. It was a close race, but it proved again that without the benefit of a mishap it was very difficult to pass a leading boat, for New Zealand went on to win.

A Critical Rounding

The fifth and last race of the challenger finals ended after a moment of high drama. Though *Stars and Stripes* was ahead around every mark, it was a cliffhanger because *New Zealand* kept diminishing the lead, constantly threatening to overtake *Stars and Stripes*. On the last downwind leg, *New Zealand* crept within a few feet of *Stars and Stripes*'s transom. *Stars and Stripes* rounded safely in the inside position and *New Zealand*, spinning around in her wake, touched the buoy and had to round again, in effect losing the race right then. Here, at the critical mark, *Stars and Stripes* is rounding just a squeak ahead of *New Zealand*.

Stern Chase

After months of close racing throughout the trials, often with the contestants only a few seconds apart, the actual America's Cup races followed a less exciting, more traditional pattern. Through the four-race series *Stars and Stripes* was ahead at every mark. Though the defender *Kookaburra III* raced valiantly, the outcome seemed inevitable from their first race. Here, in the second race, *Stars and Stripes* with Dennis Conner at the helm leads *Kookaburra III*. It was a scene that repeated itself on every windward leg. At the finish of their series, the America's Cup returned to the United States, this time across the continent to the San Diego Yacht Club.

Victory Sail

After the America's Cup was won, many of the support group boarded *Stars and Stripes* for the triumphant homeward sail into Fremantle. Clenched in some of the crew's waving hands are a few of the thousands of bottles of champagne that popped their corks in Fremantle that day.

Dennis Conner

In 1983, Dennis Conner was the first American skipper to lose the America's Cup; in 1987, off Fremantle, Western Australia, he became the first to win it back. During the 1980s, when his name was almost synonymous with America's Cup racing, the event moved from a challenge between yacht clubs to an international contest in which the competing yachts really represented countries more than clubs. It also became a highly organized multinational corporate enterprise rather than the gentlemanly challenge of tradition.

Iain Murray

Iain Murray, a champion Australian sailor and a guiding spirit in the organization and training of the *Kookaburra* team, won the right to defend the America's Cup for Australia and the Royal Perth Yacht Club. Despite his victory over the experienced Alan Bond team, the quality of the Australian defense was not very well understood at the time of the America's Cup finals. His defense was valiant, but unavailing.

Chris Dickson

Chris Dickson, skipper of *New Zealand*, was the youngest of the 12-meter skippers at Fremantle and had limited previous experience with the 12s. Nevertheless, he showed a winning style from the outset of the racing, and the most critical competition turned out to be the racing between Dickson and the veteran Dennis Conner. Dickson's fall from power was a fascinating story to all the press.

Michael Fay

Michael Fay, a merchant banker, masterminded the New Zealand challenge. He developed it into a strong contender, always ready with an astute answer to the press and an even more astute strategy overall. He turned out to be a lasting force in America's Cup racing, changing the direction intended by the San Diego Yacht Club.

Index

Note: Boldface page references refer to photographs. The page numbers refer to the position of the caption, not necessarily the photograph itself.

A

Aboard *Erin*, 1920, **42**
Adams, Charles Francis, 40, 61, 82, **83**
Aeromarine, 43
After Dawn, 203
Afterguard, 113, 186
Aldridge, 3
Aluminum, 196, 222, 227
Aluminum Frames, **227**
America, 15, 20
America, 1893, 20
America II, 256, 269
American and English Yachts Illustrated, 8
America's Cup, 250, 255, 256, 257, 269, 273, 274, 275
America's Cup buoy, 257
America's Cup Buoy off Fremantle, **257**
America's Cup finals, 260, 275
America's Cup races or series, xi, 3, 4, 6, 11, 15, 16, 23, 26, 29, 33, 36, 40, 41, 42, 43, 61, 70, 103, 124, 127, 128, 162, 180, 183, 196, 227, 240, 255, 256, 273, 275, 276
America's Cup 12-meter racing, 257
America's Cup Winners, **250**
Arabian Gulf, 255
Aries, 206
AT&T, 4
Athlon, 1884, **17**
Atlantic, 15, 36, 57, 61
Atlantic City, 43
Atlantic, 1933, **57**
Atlantic, 1929, **57**
Aurora, 39
Australia, 238, 243
Australia, 96, 208, 255, 256, 275
Australia II, 11, 196, 248, 250

Australia II Leads, **250**
Australia IV, 256
Azzurra, 255

B

Bahrein, 132
Bakelite, 166
Bantam, 62
Bark, 61
Bartram, Burr, xi
Bath Iron Works, 107
Bath, Maine, 107, 114
Battery, 9
Bavier, Bob, 188
Beam End, **198**
Beaufort, South Carolina, 43
Bell Telephone Labs, 4
"Bendy" boom, 91, 187
Bendy mast, 243
Bermuda Race, 11, 16, 54
Bermuda Racer *Micco*, 1924, **54**
Bertram, Dick, xi
Bertrand, John, 250
Black Dawn, **76**
Blackaller, Tom, 256
Bliss, Zenas, Professor, 113
Block Island, 11, 12, 15, 127, 140, 188, 212
Block Island Sound, 49, 65, 76, 167, 232, 236, 244
Bloodhound, 161
Bluenose, 44
Bolero, 161
Bolles, C. E., 3, 8
Bombard, Buddy, xi
Bond, Alan, 250, 256, 275

Boston, 36, 62, 166
Bosun's chair, 112
Bowman, 230
Bowsprit *Reliance*, 1903, 33
Brenton Reef lightship, 116
Bristol, Rhode Island, 68, 79
British Isles, 16
British Royal Yacht Squadron, 127
Broken Mast, 188, 216
Bronze plating, 66, 107
Brooklyn Bridge, 3
Brown, John Nicholas, 161
Brown Smith Jones, 62, 94
Building *Ranger*, 1937, 107
Buoy, 153
Burgess, Edward, 8
Burgess, W. Starling, 61, 68, 81, 100
Burton, J. R., 3, 8
Burton, (Sir) William, 40
Butler, Brigadier General B. F., 20
Buzzards Bay, 71, 91, 98, 109, 120, 122, 124, 161

C

Calling the Line, 230
Canada, 255
Canada II, 256, 258, 266
Capetown, 132
Cargo ships, 50
Caribbean, 208
Carrick, Robert W., 196
Carstens, Willy, 42
Challenge 12, 246
Challenge 12 and *Victory 83*, 246
Challenger of Record, 255
Champion, 140
Chesapeake Bugeye, 62, 94
Chinook, 73
Chinook, a NYYC 40, 73
Chris Dickson, 276
Christening, 162
Christening *Columbia*, 1958, 162
Chubb, Percy, xi
Circles, 1983, 244
City Hall, 4
City Island, 6, 11, 12, 49, 61, 62, 73, 76, 162, 164, 166, 206

City Island Roads, 76
Civil War, 20
Close-Hauled, 271
Closest Finish, The, 185
Clouds, 10
Coastal Cruising, 76
Coffee Grinders, The, 178, 215, 218
Colonia, 22
Columbia and *Shamrock*, 1899, 26
Columbia (gaff-rigger), 26, 29, 30, 31, 79
Columbia (12-meter), xi, 127, 162, 165, 166, 167, 169, 175
Coming About, 269
Commodore's Cup Race, 20
Commuter yacht, 80
Connecticut, 135, 161
Conner, Dennis, 242, 255, 256, 258, 273, 275, 276
Coney Island, 9
Constellation, 186, 187, 188, 190, 192
Constellation's Bendy Boom, 1964, 187
Constitution, 30
Constitution and *Columbia*, 1901, 30
Cooper Union, 3
Corsair, 80
Costa Smeralda Yacht Club, 255
Cotton Blossom II, 143
Cotton Blossom II Bow, 143
Courageous, 128, 196, 227, 229, 230, 232, 233, 234, 236, 238, 240, 255
Courageous and *Australia*, 238
Courageous's Hull, 229
Crane, Clinton H., 65
Cresting Sea, 71
Crew of *Micco*, 1924, 54
Critical Rounding, A, 272
Crosby, Bill, 62
Crossing Spinnaker Tacks, 128
Crossing Tacks I, 236
Crossing Tacks III, 260
Crossing Tacks II, 240
Cuba, 43
Cudmore, Harold, 256
Cumberland Queen, 49
Cunningham, Briggs, 162
Cup Yachts Hauled Out in Erie Basin, 1893, 22
Curtiss 5 FL, 43
Cutter, keel, 23
Cutters, 16, 151
Cythera, 19

D

Dacron, 248
Dame Pattie, 196, 218, 219, 221
Dana, Charlie, 12
Dana, Posy, 12
Dana, Richard Henry, 12
Davies, Ambassador Joseph E., 140
Davies, Mrs. Joseph E., 140
Dawn Under Mackerel Sky, 76
Day, Thomas Fleming, 15
Deck *Nedumo*, 138
Deck of *Dame Pattie*, 218
Deck of *Endeavour*, 87
Deck of *Henry Ford*, 1923, 47
Deed of Gift, 256
Defender (gaff-rigger), 16, 23, 24, 25, 79
Defender in Dry Dock, 1895, 23
Defender (12-meter), 244
Defender Under Spinnaker, 1895, 25
Defiance, 36
Dennis Conner, 275
Devereaux, Henry, 138
Dickson, Chris, 276
Diving into the Trough, 260
Dorade, 107
Doria, Hurricane, 219
Double-ender, 66
Down Under, 255
Downwind, 271
Dry dock, 23
Dry Nor'easter, 219
Dry Squall, 96
Drying Out, 175
Dunraven, Lord, 15

E

Eagle, 256, 262
Easterner, 166
Eastman, 10
Eastman Extra Rapid, 3
Eastman, George, 9
East River, 3, 5, 164
8 × 10-inch camera, 16
8 × 10-inch glass plate(s), 16, 18, 23, 24, 25, 26, 29, 33, 35, 36, 40, 49

Elizabeth Ann Howard, 46
Elizabeth Islands, 71
Elmina, 35
Emerald, 1893, 20
Endeavour, 84, 87, 92, 115, 120, 122, 124
Endeavour I and *Endeavour II*, 62
Endeavour I's Deck, 115
Endeavour II, 87, 107, 114, 115, 118, 119, 120, 122
Endeavour II Restarts, 119
End of a Race, The, 92
England, 8, 57, 73, 255
Enterprise Below Decks, 69
Enterprise Crossing *Courageous*, 1977, 234
Enterprise (J-boat), 61, 64, 65, 68, 70, 87, 111
Enterprise (12-meter), 234
Erie Basin, Brooklyn, 22, 23
Erin, 29, 41, 42
Europe, 195
Evening in Gulf Stream, 202
Execution Light, 138

F

Falconer, Bruce, 200
Falconer, Sandy, 200
Farrell Lines, 50
Fastnet Race, 107
Fay, Michael, 256, 276
Federal No. 1 (steam tug), 52
Fiberglass 12-meter, 258
Fifth Avenue, 3
Fighting Forties, 73
First Fiberglass 12, 258
Fishermen's Races, 46, 47
5 × 7-inch glass plate, 42, 47, 50, 52, 54, 62
5 × 7-inch panchromatic film, 49
5 × 7-inch Speed Graphic, 16, 41, 47, 50, 52, 54, 67, 195
Flying Fish, 71
Flying Spinnakers, 127, 132
Focal-plane shutter, 50, 52, 54, 57
Focus scales, 24
Fog, 153, 233
Fog at Buoy, 153
Fogbound, 153
Fort Lauderdale, 255
Foto, 4, 33, 67, 79, 83, 84, 91, 96, 124
Foto IV, 11, 195, 196

Foto I, 6, 10, 76
Foto III, 4, **5**, 6, 11, 62, 76, 127, 195, 196
Foto II, 11, 12, 76
4 × 5-inch Speed Graphic, 62
France, 255
Freedom, 196, 242, 243, 247
Freedom and *Australia*, **243**
Freedom and *Liberty*, **247**
Freedom, 1980, **242**
Fremantle, Western Australia, 255, 256, 263, 266,
    271, 274, 275, 276
Fremantle Doctor, 263
French Kiss, 256, 266, 269
Fried, Mr., 10
Full-rigged ships, 15, 50, 52, 61
Fulton Street, 5

G

Gaff-riggers, 31, 61
Gaff rigs, 36
Gage Roads, 255, 257
Gardner, William, 36, 57
Genoa Yacht Club, 256
Genoas, **248**
Gertrude L. Thebaud, 44
Gleam, 130, 132
Glen Cove, 39, 68, 96, 135
Gloucester Fishermen, 1923, **46**
Gloucester fishing schooner, 1938, **44**
Gloucester, Massachusetts, 44
Goat Island, 196
Good News, **161**
Graphlex camera, 42
Gravesend Bay, 16
Great Isaac Light, 202
Greeley Square, 4
Gretel, 127, 167, 172, 173, 175, **177**, 179, 180,
    183, 184, 185
Gretel Chasing *Weatherly*, **183**
Gretel in a Northeaster, 1962, **172**
Gretel in a Squall, **173**
Gretel Passing *Weatherly*, **180**
Gretel Surfing, **180**
Gucci, 256
Gulf Stream, 107, 157, 202
Gundlach camera, 3

H

Hacker, runabout, 11
Haff, Captain Hank, 24
Hand-held camera, 24
Hare, Jimmy, 3
Harlem River, 5
Hawaii, 195, 208, 256
Heading East, **161**
Heart of America, 256, 263, 269
Hell Gate, 5
Hemment, J. C., 8
Henry Ford, 46, 47
Herald, the (newspaper), 26
Herbulot spinnaker, 169
Heritage, 196, 225
Herreshoff, L. Francis, 66, 157
Herreshoff, Nathaniel, 16, 22, 23, 25, 27, 39, 6
    73
Herreshoff yard, 68, 79, 107
Heywood, John, 188
Highball Express, The, 1920, **43**
Hiking Out IV, **201**
Hiking Out I, **200**
Hiking Out III, **201**
Hiking Out II, **200**
Hinman, George, xi
History of the New York Yacht Club, 70
Hoisting *Ranger*'s Main, **112**
Hoisting the Mainsail Aboard *Defender*, 1895, **24**
Hood, Ted, xi, 187
Hovey, Chandler, 103
H.S. Whiton, 49
Hudson River, 5
Huntington Harbor, 105
Hussar, 61

I

Iain Murray, **275**
Independence (graff-rigger), 30
Independence (12-meter), 236, 240
Indian Ocean, 255, 258
Ingomar, 35
Ingomar and *Elmina*, 1907, **35**
International Fishermen's Races, 44
International Knockdown, **145**

International One Designs, 127, 128, 144, 145, 146, 147, 197
Internationals Crossing Tacks, **144**
International Spinnakers, **148**
International Start, **147**
Intrepid, xi, 196, 213, 215, 216, 218, 219, 221, 222, 225, 227, 230, 234
Intrepid, Courageous, **227**
Intrepid's Deck, **215**
Inverness, **206**
Iroquois, 1886, **19**
Isbrandtsen, Jakob, xi
Istalena, 39
Italia, 256
Italy, 255

J

J-boats, 36, 61, 62, 66, 70, 79, 80, 91, 114, 116, 122, 124, 135, 162, 180
J-Boats in the Fog, **124**
J-Class yachts, 6, 103, 127
Jacksonville, Florida, 20
Jib-headed rig, 36
Jibe Set in Shadow, **264**
Jibe Set in Sun, **264**
Johnston, J. S., 8
Joseph Conrad, 62, **105**
Jubilee, 22
Julie, 151

K

K Class, 1907, **39**
Kaiser's Cup Race, 57
Kennedy, Joseph, 42
Kennedy, President John F., 42
Kennedy, Rose, 42
Ketch, 76, 206
Ketch, centerboard, 54, 94
Kevlar, 248
Key West, 43
Khan, Aga, 255
Kialoa, **208**
Knapp, Arthur, 113
Knockdown, **216**

Kodachrome, 9, 62
Kolius, John, 256
Kookaburra, 275
Kookaburra III, 256, 260, 273

L

Lake Michigan, 256
Larchmont, 3, 9, 127, 128, 137
Lardner, Ring, 70
Lawley yard, 66
Leaches, **210**
Lee, Robert E., 12
Lens, short-focus, 24
Lens, stopped-down, 23
Lens stops, 24
Lens, wide-angle, 47, 157
Levick, Edwin, 5
Liberty, 196, 244, 247, 248, 250
Life magazine, 9, 127, 132
Lifting Out, **262**
Lionheart, 243
Lipton, Sir Thomas, 15, 29, 40, 42, 62, 70, 234
Lockwood, Luke, xi
Long Island, 148
Long Island Sound, 6, 39, 73, 76, 96, 128, 138, 147, 154
Lord, Frederick K., 11
Louis Vuitton Cup, 256
Louis Vuitton Fleet Race, 257
Luders 16s, 154, 155, 166

M

M-boats, **96**
McCullough, Commodore Robert, 206
Magic Carpet, **205**
Manganese bronze plating, 23
Manhattan, 11, 16, 138
Marblehead, 4, 11
Marble House, 250
Marconi rig, 36
Marconi wireless telegraphy, 26
Marseilles, 205
Martha's Vineyard, 96
Matthews, Dick, xi

Matthews, Don, xi
Maxi ocean racers, 124, 195, 206, 208
Maxi ocean-racing yachts, 255
Mediterranean, 205, 208
Melges, Buddy, 256
Merry Maiden, 151
Miami, Florida, 43
Miami-Nassau Race, 107, 157, 202
Michael Fay, **276**
Micco, 16, **54**
Micco crew, 54
Migrant, 61, 62, 92
Migrant Headsails, **92**
Mistral, 205
Mizzen, 151
Montauk Point, 76, 140
Morgan, Harry, xi
Morgan, J. Pierpont, 80
Morgan, Junius S., 65, 80
Mosbacher, Emil "Bus," Jr., xi, 162, 176, 196, **215,**
    216, 219
Motor drives, 195
Mouette, **73**
Multihulls, 255
Multispeed between-the-lens shutter, 36
Multispeed shutter, 18, 57
Murray, Iain, 275
Mustang Reefing Main, **148**
Mylar, 248
Mylar and Kevlar, **248**
Mystic, Connecticut, 7
Mystic Seaport Museum, 7

N

Nassau, 206
Nassau Street, 4, 61
National Association of Engine and Boat
    Manufacturers, 7
Navigator, The, **157**
Nedumo, 138
Nefertiti, 175, 186, 187
Nefertiti's Spinnaker Staysail, **186**
Nevins yard, 62, 73, 162
New England, 16, 172, 219
New London, 122, 135, 188
New Rochelle, 73

New York, 4, 5, 7, 11, 16, 22, 41, 43, 50, 52, 57,
    62, 162, 166
New York Bay, 15
New York harbor, 26, 105, 164
New York Telephone, 4
New York Yacht Club, xi, 6, 29, 40, 73, 80, 107,
    127, 250
New York Yacht Club Annual Cruise, 122
New York Yacht Club 50s, 16, 39
New York Yacht Club 50s, 1913, 39
New York Yacht Club Squadron, 15
New York Yacht Club 32-footers, 62, 148
New Zealand, 256, 258, 264, 266, 269, 271, 272,
    276
New Zealand, 255
Newport, Rhode Island, xi, 6, 42, 62, 79, 98, 103,
    109, 114, 115, 140, 161, 167, 173, 175, 183,
    188, 196, 238, 241, 250, 257
Newport Beach, 256
Newport shipyard, 175
Newport-to-Bermuda Race, 148
Newspaper Row, 4, 16
Nichols, George, 65
Nightwind, 135
Nina, 96, **100**
North Carolina, 4
Northeaster, 172, 188
Northeaster, 188
Northern Light, 130, 132
Norway, 107
Nova Scotia schooner-yacht, 62
Noyes, Brad, xi
Nyala, 128, 132

O

Ostar fleet, 12
Off Soundings, 153
Off the Wind, **122**
Ohonkaya, 58
Olympics, 255
On the Wind, **120**
On the Wind's Highway, 111
Optimist Pram, 195
Orthochromatic negative, 10, 36
Oyster Bay, 39

P

Paine, John B., 22
Panchromatic emulsion, 36
Panchromatic negative, 10
Paradise Island, 206
Park Avenue boom, 87
Parkinson, John, Jr., 61, 70
Parry, Kevin, 256
Payne, Alan, 175
Penguin, 195, 198
Perfect Sailing Weather, **157**
Philip, Prince, 161
Point Judith, 71, 111
Port Jibe, **190**
Powerful 12, A, **175**
Prestige, 96
Prohibition, 43, 61
Pyro developer, 35

Q

Quadrilateral jib, 109, 111
Quarter plate, 3¼ × 4¼-inch, instantaneous, 22
Queen Mab, **98**

R

Rain, **154**
Rainbow, 61, 62, 79, 80, 81, 82, 87, 88, **91**, 92,
    103, 111, **114**, **116**, 120, 122, 124
Rainbow Launching, 1934, **79**
Rainbow Stern, **91**
Rainsquall Finish, **137**
Ranger, 61, 62, 107, **109**, 111, 112, 113, **114**, **116**,
    118, 119, 120, 122, 124
Ranger and Lumber Schooner, **122**
Ranger on the Wind, **111**
Ranger's Afterguard, **113**
Ranger's Bow, **109**
Raven, 31, **150**
Reaching, **266**
Red Bank dory, 11
Reflex camera, 9, 25
Reliance, 15, 33, 79

Reliance, 1903, **33**
Resolute, 16, 40, 79
Resolute, 1914, **36**
Rhode Island, 94, 98
Riding a Swell, **94**
Rio de Janeiro, 132
Rita Irene, 62, **105**
Ritter, Eric, 187
Roaring Forties, 73
Roosevelt, President Franklin Delano, 6
Rosenfeld, David, 6
Rosenfeld, Eleanor, 6
Rosenfeld, Esther, 7
Rosenfeld, Jonathan, 7
Rosenfeld, Morris, xi, 3, 4, 6, 7
Rosenfeld, Richard, 7
Rosenfeld, Ruth, 7, 196
Rosenfeld, Stanley, xi, 3
Rosenfeld, William, 6
Round Robin, 255
Round-the-buoy racing, 127
Rounding the Jibe Mark, **266**
Royal Perth Yacht Club, 257
Rudder magazine, 15
Russia, 140

S

Sail Change, **179**
San Diego Yacht Club, 256, 273, 276
San Francisco, 256
Sandbagger, The, 1893, **18**
Sandbaggers, 15
Sandy Hook lightship, 26
Saraband, **98**, 161
Scandinavia, 73
Sceptre, 127, 164, **165**, 169
Sceptre and *Columbia*, **169**
Sceptre Weather, **169**
Sceptre's Underbody, **165**
Schooner, four-masted, 49, 122
Schooner, lumber, 122
Schooner-rigged, 36
Schooner, staysail, 94, 100
Schooner, steel, 19
Schooner, three-masted, 57, 61
Schooners, 35
Schooners, fishing, 15

Schooners, working, 15, 49
Scotland, 73
Scow, 23
Scow-type, 33
Scribner's Sons, Charles, 8
Sea Cloud, 61, 127, **140**
Sears, Commodore Henry, 162
Sears, Mary, 162
Settling into the Trough, **263**
Seven Seas, 61
Shakespeare, 169
Shamrock, 26, 29
Shamrock and *Columbia*, 1899, **29**
Shamrock and *Erin*, 1899, **29**
Shamrock V, 62, **70**
Shamrock IV, **41**
Shamrock IV Deck View, 1920, **41**
Shamrock III, 33
Shamrock II, **31**
Shamrock II and *Columbia*, 1901, **31**
Sheu, Larry, xi
Shutter speed, 35
Shuttle, 80
6½ × 8½-inch glass plate, 39, 49
6½ × 8½-inch (negative) format, 16
Skipjacks, 94
Sloop, auxiliary cruising, 148
Sloop, cruising/racing, 127
Sloop, Raven class, 150
Sloops, 16, 17, 22
Sloops, jib-headed, 61, 64
Smashing Through, **262**
Snipe, 62
Soft Glow, **225**
Sopwith Camel, 62
Sopwith, Mrs. T.O.M., 84
Sopwith, T.O.M., 62, 84, 87, 115
South Boston, 66
Southern Cross, 128, 232, 233
Southern Cross and *Courageous* in Mist, **232**
Southern Ocean Racing Conference, 62, 206
Sovereign, **190**, 192
Spain, 100
Sparkman & Stephens, 62, 162
Spectators, 80
Speed Graphic, 9
Spinnaker Release, **269**
Spinnaker Trouble, **263**
Spinnakers, 132, 210
Squall, **155**, 173, 216

Square-rigger, 105
St. Francis Yacht Club, 256
Staats-Zeitung (newspaper), 3
Stake boat, 25
Stamford, Connecticut, 166
Starboard Tack, **197**
Star class, 36
Stars and Stripes, 256, 258, 260, 263, 264, 271, 272, 273, 274
Start, **192**
Start, Final Race, **118**
Start, 1920 America's Cup, *Resolute* and *Shamrock IV*, **40**
Start Schooners, 1921, **58**
Stebbins, N. L., 8
Steel frames, 66, 107
Steel hull, 22
Steel plates, flush-riveted, 107
Stephens, Olin, 61, 107, 113, 127, 165
Stephens, Rod, 62, 107, 113, 148, 162, 188
Stern Chase, **273**
Stevens Institute, 196, 213
Stewart, W. A. W., xi
Stormy Weather, **107**
St. Roque, 12
Sturrock, Jock, 173, 175, **184**
Sunset, **234**
Surfing, 180
Sverige, **236**
Swell, A., **167**

T

Tabarly, Eric, 57
Ted Turner at the Helm, **241**
35mm camera, 9, 62, 127, 128, 157, 195, 197
Ticonderoga, **157**
Titanium Tension, **222**
Towing tank, 196
Towing Tank, 1966, **213**
Tripod-mounted camera, 8, 24
Trouble, **151**
Turner, Ted, 196, 234, 238, **241**
Tusitala, 1925, **50**
Tusitala Under Tow, 1925, **52**
12-Meters Around the Buoys, **135**
Twelve-meter class, 135
12-Meter Spinnakers, **130**

Twelve-meter yachts, 73, 127, 162, 213, 216, 240, 255, 258, 260, 262, 276
2¼ × 3¼-inch negative, 195
Two Years Before the Mast, 12

U

Under *Endeavour*, 84
Underbody, 165
United States, 7, 8, 41, 73, 255, 273
Unloading *Sceptre*, **164**
USA, 256, 260
U.S.S. Joseph P. Kennedy, Jr., 42

V

Valkyrie, 127, **148**
Valkyrie, 1946, **148**
Valkyrie III, 23, 25
Vanderbilt, Harold S., 61, 62, 69, 80, 81, 82, 87, 107, 111, 113, 118
Vanderbilt, Mike, xi
Vanderbilt, Mrs. Harold, 113
Vanitie, 16, 36, 111
Vanitie, 1914, **36**
Victory 83, 246
Victory Sail, **274**
View camera, 23
Vigilant, 22, 79
Vim, xi, 162
Vinky, 150

W

Wall Street, 61
Water Gypsy, 96

Water-jet-powered yachts, 255
Weatherly, xi, 127, 166, 167, 175, 176, 177, 178, 180, 183, 184, 185, 215
Weatherly in Frame, **166**
Weatherly Lifting, **176**
Weetamoe, 64, **65**, 79, 103, 111
Weetamoe's Deck, **103**
Weetamoe's Spinnaker, **79**
Western Australia, 255
Western Electric, 4
Whirlwind, 64, **66**, 67
White Crusader, 256
Wind on the Water, 258
Windward, 96
Windward Work, **221**
Winged Keel, **250**
Winsome, 39
Wooden Hull, 66, 143
Wooden 12-meters, 143, 166, 175, 227
Working Schooners, 1906–1928, **49**
World War I, 36, 39, 41, 62
World War II, 7, 9, 61, 127, 140
Wratten and Wainright, 3, 36
Wright Brothers, 4

Y

Yankee, 61, 62, 81, 82, 83, 88, 103, 120, 122
Yankee, 1930, **62**
Yankee, *Rainbow* Crossing Tacks, **88**
Yawl, 138, 151, 161, 205

Z

Zio, 135
Zio and *Nightwind*, **135**